The Open University

D0994608

A103
AN INTRODUCTION TO
THE HUMANITIES

Resource
Book 1

The Open University
Walton Hall, Milton Keynes MK7 6AA

First published 1997. Reprinted 1998, 1999, 2000, 2001, 2002, 2003

Edited, designed and typeset by The Open University.

Printed and bound in Great Britain by The Bath Press, Bath

ISBN 0 7492 8710 1

This text is a component of the Open University course A103 *An Introduction to the Humanities*. Details of this and other Open University courses are available from Course Enquiries Data Service, PO Box 625, Dane Road, Milton Keynes MK1 1TY; telephone + 44 - (0)1908 858585.

1.7

31614B/a103rb1i1.7

CONTENTS

PREFACE

Four resource books accompany A103 *An Introduction to the Humanities*. *Resource Book 1* provides supporting material for Blocks 1 and 2, *Resource Book 2* for Block 3, *Resource Book 3* for Blocks 4 and 5, and *Resource Book 4* for Block 6.

The resource books are not intended to be free-standing readers which make sense on their own; they serve the teaching needs of the course. Your path through the material in the resource books and the pace at which you work are set by the course units. In the units, as occasion demands, you will find instructions to turn to one or other of the resource books. In broadcast notes or on audio-cassettes you may also be referred to specific sections of the resource books.

When you are asked to read a text, make sure you do so carefully – unless you are told otherwise in the unit, this material is not an optional extra but an essential part of your study. The amount of material related to each week's work varies according to the requirements of the subject. But in all cases the total workload for the week should not exceed fifteen hours. Where there is *more* material in a resource book than your week's work calls for, this is to provide additional material for TMAs during the lifetime of the course.

The resource books are organized into sections with each item given an identifying number, A1, A2 and so on. Instructions to read material in the resource books will refer to this information.

Because the resource books have been prepared to meet the needs of A103 students, some items have been edited to remove inessential material, sometimes including footnotes. Where text has been removed this is indicated by an ellipsis in square brackets: [···]. Additional comments or pieces of information which are not part of the original text are generally placed within square brackets. In the poetry section in *Resource Book 1* the meanings of selected words are glossed under the poems.

Section A FORM AND MEANING IN POETRY: THE SONNET

A1 Petrarch, 'Blest be the day, and blest the month, the year'

From Thomas G. Bergin (ed.) (1954) *The Rhymes of Francesco Petrarca*, Edinburgh, Oliver and Boyd, p.16.

Blest be the day, and blest the month, the year,
The spring, the hour, the very moment blest,
The lovely scene, the spot, where first oppress'd
I sunk, of two bright eyes the prisoner:
And blest the first soft pang, to me most dear,
Which thrill'd my heart, when Love became its guest;
And blest the bow, the shafts which pierced my breast,
And even the wounds, which bosom'd thence I bear.
Blest too the strains which, pour'd through glade and grove,
Have made the woodlands echo with her name;
The sighs, the tears, the languishment, the love:
And blest those sonnets, sources of my fame;
And blest that thought – Oh! never to remove!
Which turns to her alone, from her alone which came.

A2 Sir Thomas Wyatt (1503–42), 'Farewell, Love'

From D.M. Main (ed.) (1880) *A Treasury of English Sonnets*, Manchester, Alexander Ireland and Co., p.1.

Farewell, Love, and all thy laws for ever!
Thy baited hooks shall tangle me no more:
Senec and Plato call me from thy lore
To perfect wealth my wit for to endeavour.
In blind error when I did perséver,
Thy sharp repulse, that pricketh aye so sore,
Taught me in trifles that I set no store;
But 'scaped forth thence, since, liberty is lever.
Therefore, farewell! go trouble younger hearts.
And in me claim no more authority:
With idle youth go use thy property,
And thereon spend thy many brittle darts;
For hitherto though I have lost my time,
Me list no longer rotten boughs to climb.

Senec: an abbreviation of Seneca, Roman statesman, philosopher and writer.
Plato: renowned Greek philosopher.
list: in the archaic sense of 'care' or 'desire'.

A3 Sir Thomas Wyatt, 'Whoso list to hunt'

From G. Bullett (ed.) (1966) *Silver Poets of the Sixteenth Century*, London, Everyman's Library, Dent (first published 1947), p.3.

Whoso list to hunt, I know where is an hind, *A*
But as for me, helas, I may no more. *B*
The vain travail hath wearied me so sore, *B*
I am of them that farthest come behind. *A*
Yet may I by no means my wearied mind *A*
Draw from the Deer, but as she fleeth afore *B*
Fainting I follow. I leave off therefore, *B*
Since in a net I seek to hold the wind. *A*
Who list her hunt (I put him out of doubt) *C*
As well as I may spend his time in vain. *D*
And graven with diamonds in letters plain *D*
There is written her fair neck round about: *C*
'Noli me tangere, for Caesar's I am, *e*
And wild for to hold, though I seem tame.' *e*

list: wishes, or likes.

Noli me tangere: 'touch me not'.

A4 Henry Howard, Earl of Surrey (1516–47), 'Set me whereas the sun doth parch the green'

From G. Bullett (ed.) (1966) *Silver Poets of the Sixteenth Century*, London, Everyman's Library, Dent (first published 1947), p.120.

Set me whereas the sun doth parch the green,
Or where his beams may not dissolve the ice,
In temperate heat, where he is felt and seen;
With proud people, in presence sad and wise;
Set me in low, or yet in high degree;
In the long night, or in the shortest day;
In clear weather, or where clouds thickest be;
In lusty youth, or when my hairs be gray:
Set me in earth, in heaven, or yet in hell,
In hill, in dale, or in the foaming flood;
Thrall, or at large, alive whereso I dwell,
Sick, or in health, in ill fame or in good,
Yours will I be, and with this only thought
Comfort myself when that my hope is nought.

A5 Henry Howard, Earl of Surrey, 'The golden gift that Nature did thee give'

From G. Bullett (ed.) (1966) *Silver Poets of the Sixteenth Century*, London, Everyman's Library, Dent (first published 1947), p.121.

The golden gift that Nature did thee give,
To fasten friends and feed them at thy will
With form and favour, taught me to believe
How thou art made to show her greatest skill,
Whose hidden virtues are not so unknown
But lively dooms might gather at the first:
Where beauty so her perfect seed hath sown,
Of other graces follow needs there must.
Now certes, lady, since all this is true,
That from above thy gifts are thus elect,
Do not deface them then with fancies new,
Nor change of minds, let not the mind infect:
But mercy him thy friend that doth thee serve,
Who seeks alway thine honour to preserve.

A6 Sir Walter Raleigh (1552–1618), 'To his Son'

From E. Jones (ed.) (1991) *The New Oxford Book of Sixteenth Century Verse*, Oxford, Oxford University Press, p.369.

Three things there be that prosper up apace,
And flourish, whilst they grow asunder far,
But on a day, they meet all in one place,
And when they meet they one another mar.
And they be these: the wood, the weed, the wag.
The wood is that, which makes the gallow tree;
The weed is that, which strings the hangman's bag;
The wag, my pretty knave, betokeneth thee.
Mark well, dear boy, whilst these assemble not,
Green springs the tree, hemp grows, the wag is wild;
But when they meet, it makes the timber rot,
It frets the halter, and it chokes the child.
    Then bless thee, and beware, and let us pray,
    We part not with thee at this meeting day.

weed: hempweed, or 'hemp', for making cord.
wag: a mischievous boy.

A7 Edmund Spenser (1552–99), 'One day I wrote her name upon the strand'

From D.M. Main (ed.) (1880) *A Treasury of English Sonnets*, Manchester, Alexander Ireland and Co., p.12.

One day I wrote her name upon the strand;
But came the waves and washèd it away:
Again I wrote it with a second hand,
But came the tide and made my pains his prey.
Vain man! said she, that dost in vain assay
A mortal thing so to immortalize;
For I myself shall like to this decay,
And eke my name be wipèd out likewise.
Not so, quoth I; let baser things devise
To die in dust, but you shall live by fame:
My verse your virtues rare shall eternize,
And in the heavens write your glorious name, –
Where, whenas death shall all the world subdue,
Our love shall live, and later life renew.

assay: attempt.

eke: also.

eternize: eternalize.

A8 Edmund Spenser, 'This holy season, fit to fast and pray'

From D.M. Main (ed.) (1880) *A Treasury of English Sonnets*, Manchester, Alexander Ireland and Co., p.6.

This holy season, fit to fast and pray,
Men to devotion ought to be inclined:
Therefore I likewise on so holy day
For my sweet Saint some service fit will find.
Her temple fair is built within my mind,
In which her glorious image placèd is,
On which my thoughts do day and night attend,
Like sacred priests that never think amiss!
There I to her, as th' author of my bliss,
Will build an altar to appease her ire,
And on the same my heart will sacrifice,
Burning in flames of pure and chaste desire:
The which vouchsafe, O goddess, to accept,
Amongst thy dearest relics to be kept.

ire: anger.
vouchsafe: grant permission.

A9 Sir Philip Sidney (1554–86), 'With how sad steps, O Moon, thou climb'st the skies!'

From P. Negri (ed.) (1994) *Great Sonnets*, New York, Dover Publications Inc., p.7.

With how sad steps, O Moon, thou climb'st the skies!
How silently, and with how wan a face!
What! may it be that even in heavenly place
That busy archer his sharp arrows tries?
Sure, if that long-with-love-acquainted eyes
Can judge of love, thou feel'st a lover's case:
I read it in thy looks; thy languish'd grace
To me that feel the like, thy state descries.
Then, even of fellowship, O Moon, tell me
Is constant love deem'd there but want of wit?
Are beauties there as proud as here they be?
Do they above love to be loved, and yet
    Those lovers scorn whom that love doth possess?
    Do they call 'virtue' there – ungratefulness?

archer: Cupid, the god of love.
languish'd: enfeebled, or tired.
descries: describes, or tells.
above: in the heavens.

A10 Sir Philip Sidney, 'The Bargain'

From E. Jones (ed.) (1991) *The New Oxford Book of Sixteenth Century Verse*, Oxford, Oxford University Press, p.298.

My true love hath my heart, and I have his,
By just exchange one for the other given.
I hold his dear, and mine he cannot miss:
There never was a better bargain driven.
His heart in me keeps me and him in one;
My heart in him his thoughts and senses guides;
He loves my heart, for once it was his own;
I cherish his, because in me it bides.
His heart his wound received from my sight;
My heart was wounded with his wounded heart;
For as from me on him his hurt did light,
So still, methought, in me his hurt did smart;
   Both equal hurt, in this change sought our bliss:
   My true love hath my heart, and I have his.

smart: sting.

A11 William Shakespeare (1564–1616), 'Weary with toil I haste me to my bed'

From M. Dodsworth (ed.) (1976) *William Shakespeare, the Sonnets and a Lover's Complaint*, London, Everyman, Sonnet 27, p.29.

Weary with toil I haste me to my bed,
The dear repose for limbs with travel tir'd;
But then begins a journey in my head
To work my mind when body's work's expir'd;
For then my thoughts, from far where I abide,
Intend a zealous pilgrimage to thee,
And keep my drooping eyelids open wide,
Looking on darkness which the blind do see:
Save that my soul's imaginary sight
Presents thy shadow to my sightless view,
Which like a jewel hung in ghastly night
Makes black night beauteous and her old face new.
   Lo, thus by day my limbs, by night my mind,
   For thee, and for myself, no quiet find.

A12 William Shakespeare, 'When, in disgrace with Fortune and men's eyes'

From M. Dodsworth (ed.) (1976) *William Shakespeare, the Sonnets and a Lover's Complaint*, London, Everyman, Sonnet 29, p.31.

When, in disgrace with Fortune and men's eyes,
I all alone beweep my outcast state,
And trouble deaf heaven with my bootless cries,
And look upon myself and curse my fate,
Wishing me like to one more rich in hope,
Featur'd like him, like him with friends possess'd,
Desiring this man's art and that man's scope,
With what I most enjoy contented least:
Yet in these thoughts myself almost despising,
Haply I think on thee, and then my state,
Like to the lark at break of day arising,
From sullen earth sings hymns at heaven's gate;
    For thy sweet love remember'd such wealth brings
    That then I scorn to change my state with kings.

bootless: pointless.
art: skill.
haply: by chance.
sullen: dark and sorrowful.

A13 William Shakespeare, 'What is your substance, whereof are you made?'

From M. Dodsworth (ed.) (1976) *William Shakespeare, the Sonnets and a Lover's Complaint*, London, Everyman, Sonnet 53, p.55.

What is your substance, whereof are you made,
That millions of strange shadows on you tend?
Since everyone hath, every one, one shade,
And you, but one, can every shadow lend.
Describe Adonis, and the counterfeit
Is poorly imitated after you;
On Helen's cheek all art of beauty set,
And you in Grecian tires are painted new.
Speak of the spring and foison of the year:
The one doth shadow of your beauty show,
The other as your bounty doth appear;
And you in every blessed shape we know.
 In all external grace you have some part,
 But you like none, none you, for constant heart.

shadows: likenesses of other people.
on you tend: wait on you.
can every shadow lend: have many attributes.
Adonis: Greek hero, the favourite of Venus.
Helen: Helen of Troy, famed for her beauty.
Grecian tires: Greek costume.
foison: harvest.

A14 William Shakespeare, 'Like as the waves make towards the pebbled shore'

From M. Dodsworth (ed.) (1976) *William Shakespeare, the Sonnets and a Lover's Complaint*, London, Everyman, Sonnet 60, p.62.

Like as the waves make towards the pebbled shore,
So do our minutes hasten to their end;
Each changing place with that which goes before,
In scquent toil all forwards do contend.
Nativity, once in the main of light,
Crawls to maturity, wherewith being crown'd
Crooked eclipses 'gainst his glory fight,
And Time that gave doth now his gift confound.
Time doth transfix the flourish set on youth
And delves the parallels in beauty's brow,
Feeds on the rarities of nature's truth,
And nothing stands but for his scythe to mow.
    And yet to times in hope my verse shall stand,
    Praising thy worth despite his cruel hand.

in sequent toil: struggling one after another.

contend: strive.

once in the main of light: having come into the world, as if afloat on a channel of light.

crooked: malignant.

transfix: impale.

delves the parallels: digs the lines.

the rarities of nature's truth: the finest things in nature's perfection.

times in hope: times only dreamt of as yet.

A15 William Shakespeare, 'Since brass, nor stone, nor earth, nor boundless sea'

From M. Dodsworth (ed.) (1976) *William Shakespeare, the Sonnets and a Lover's Complaint*, London, Everyman, Sonnet 65, p.67.

Since brass, nor stone, nor earth, nor boundless sea,
But sad mortality o'ersways their power,
How with this rage shall beauty hold a plea,
Whose action is no stronger than a flower?
O, how shall summer's honey breath hold out
Against the wrackful siege of batt'ring days
When rocks impregnable are not so stout,
Nor gates of steel so strong, but Time decays?
O fearful meditation! Where, alack,
Shall Time's best jewel from Time's chest lie hid,
Or what strong hand can hold his swift foot back,
Or who his spoil of beauty can forbid?
　　O, none, unless this miracle have might,
　　That in black ink my love may still shine bright.

since: since there is neither.
o'ersways: overrules.
hold a plea: uphold a lawsuit.
action: case at law.
spoil: destruction.

A16 William Shakespeare, 'No longer mourn for me when I am dead'

From M. Dodsworth (ed.) (1976) *William Shakespeare, the Sonnets and a Lover's Complaint*, London, Everyman, Sonnet 71, p.73.

No longer mourn for me when I am dead
Than you shall hear the surly sullen bell
Give warning to the world that I am fled
From this vile world, with vilest worms to dwell.
Nay, if you read this line, remember not
The hand that writ it; for I love you so
That I in your sweet thoughts would be forgot
If thinking on me then should make you woe.
O, if, I say, you look upon this verse
When I perhaps compounded am with clay,
Do not so much as my poor name rehearse,
But let your love even with my life decay,
  Lest the wise world should look into your moan,
  And mock you with me after I am gone.

rehearse: repeat.
moan: sorrow.

A17 William Shakespeare, 'That time of year thou mayst in me behold'

From M. Dodsworth (ed.) (1976) *William Shakespeare, the Sonnets and a Lover's Complaint*, London, Everyman, Sonnet 73, p.75.

That time of year thou mayst in me behold
When yellow leaves, or none, or few, do hang
Upon those boughs which shake against the cold,
Bare ruin'd choirs where late the sweet birds sang.
In me thou seest the twilight of such day
As after sunset fadeth in the west;
Which by and by black night doth take away,
Death's second self, that seals up all in rest.
In me thou seest the glowing of such fire
That on the ashes of his youth doth lie,
As the death-bed whereon it must expire,
Consum'd with that which it was nourish'd by.
   This thou perceiv'st, which makes thy love more strong,
   To love that well which thou must leave ere long.

choirs: churches, where divine service is sung.
seals up: as in a coffin.
his: its.

A18   William Shakespeare, 'Let me not to the marriage of true minds'

From M. Dodsworth (ed.) (1976) *William Shakespeare, the Sonnets and a Lover's Complaint*, London, Everyman, Sonnet 116, p.118.

Let me not to the marriage of true minds
Admit impediments. Love is not love
Which alters when it alteration finds,
Or bends with the remover to remove.
O no, it is an ever-fixed mark
That looks on tempests and is never shaken;
It is the star to every wand'ring bark,
Whose worth's unknown although his height be taken.
Love's not Time's fool, though rosy lips and cheeks
Within his bending sickle's compass come;
Love alters not with his brief hours and weeks,
But bears it out even to the edge of doom.
  If this be error and upon me prov'd,
  I never writ, nor no man ever lov'd.

bark: boat.
the edge of doom: judgement day.

A19   William Shakespeare, 'My mistress' eyes are nothing like the sun'

From M. Dodsworth (ed.) (1976) *William Shakespeare, the Sonnets and a Lover's Complaint*, London, Everyman, Sonnet 130, p.132.

My mistress' eyes are nothing like the sun;
Coral is far more red than her lips' red.
If snow be white, why then her breasts are dun;
If hairs be wires, black wires grow on her head.
I have seen roses damask'd, red and white,
But no such roses see I in her cheeks;
And in some perfumes is there more delight
Than in her breath that from my mistress reeks.
I love to hear her speak, yet well I know
That music hath a far more pleasing sound.
I grant I never saw a goddess go:
My mistress when she walks treads on the ground.
   And yet, by heaven, I think my love as rare
   As any she belied with false compare.

dun: dull; greyish-brown.

damask'd: mingling red and white.

A20   John Donne (1572–1631), 'Death, be not proud'

From R. Nye (ed.) (1976) *The Faber Book of Sonnets*, London, Faber and Faber, p.82.

Death, be not proud, though some have called thee
Mighty and dreadful, for thou art not so;
For those whom thou think'st thou dost overthrow
Die not, poor Death; nor yet canst thou kill me.
From rest and sleep, which but thy pictures be,
Much pleasure: then from thee much more must flow;
And soonest our best men with thee do go –
Rest of their bones and souls' delivery!
Thou'rt slave to fate, chance, kings and desperate men,
And dost with poison, war, and sickness dwell;
And poppy or charms can make us sleep as well,
And better than thy stroke. Why swell'st thou then?
One short sleep past, we wake eternally,
And death shall be no more: Death, thou shalt die.

A21　John Donne, 'At the round earth's imagin'd corners, blow'

From R. Nye (ed.) (1976) *The Faber Book of Sonnets*, London, Faber and Faber, p.81.

At the round earth's imagin'd corners, blow
Your trumpets, angels, and arise, arise
From death, you numberless infinities
Of souls, and to your scatter'd bodies go,
All whom the flood did, and fire shall o'erthrow,
All whom war, dearth, age, agues, tyrannies,
Despair, law, chance, hath slain, and you whose eyes
Shall behold God, and never taste death's woe.
But let them sleep, Lord, and me mourn a space,
For, if above all these, my sins abound,
'Tis late to ask abundance of thy grace,
When we are there. Here, on this lowly ground,
Teach me how to repent; for that's as good
As if thou hadst seal'd my pardon, with thy blood.

dearth: shortages; scarcity of food.
agues: fevers.

A22 George Herbert (1593–1633), 'Redemption'

From R. Nye (ed.) (1976) *The Faber Book of Sonnets*, London, Faber and Faber, p.91.

Having been tenant long to a rich Lord,
    Not thriving, I resolved to be bold,
    And made a suit unto him, to afford
A new small-rented lease, and cancel th' old.

In Heaven at his manor I him sought:
    They told me there, that he was lately gone
    About some land, which he had dearly bought
Long since on earth, to take possession.

I straight return'd, and knowing his great birth,
    Sought him accordingly in great resorts;
    In cities, theatres, gardens, parks and courts:
At length I heard a ragged noise and mirth

    Of thieves and murderers: there I him espied,
    Who straight, *Your suit is granted*, said, and died.

suit: petition.

A23 George Herbert, 'The Answer'

From R. Nye (ed.) (1976) *The Faber Book of Sonnets*, London, Faber and Faber, p.92.

My comforts drop and melt away like snow:
I shake my head, and all the thoughts and ends,
Which my fierce youth did bandy, fall and flow
Like leaves about me, or like summer friends,
Flies of estates and sunshine. But to all,
Who think me eager, hot, and undertaking,
But in my prosecutions slack and small;
As a young exhalation, newly waking,
Scorns his first bed of dirt, and means the sky;
But cooling by the way, grows pursy and slow,
And settling to a cloud, doth live and die
In that dark state of tears: to all, that so
Show me, and set me, I have one reply,
Which they that know the rest, know more than I.

exhalation: mist, or vapour.

means the sky: aspires upwards.

pursy: short-winded; out of breath.

A24 John Milton (1608–74), 'To the Lord General Cromwell, May 1652: On the Proposals of Certain Ministers at the Committee for Propagation of the Gospel'

From D.M. Main (ed.) (1880) *A Treasury of English Sonnets*, Manchester, Alexander Ireland and Co., p.74.

(Public decoration)

Cromwell, our chief of men, who through a cloud A
Not of war only, but detractions rude, B
Guided by faith and matchless fortitude, B
To peace and truth thy glorious way hast ploughed, A
And on the neck of crownèd Fortune proud A
Hast reared God's trophies, and his work pursued; B
While Darwen stream, with blood of Scots imbrued, B
And Dunbar field resounds thy praises loud, A
And Worcester's laureate wreath: yet much remains C
To conquer still; Peace hath her victories A
No less renowned than War: new foes arise, C
Threatening to bind our souls with secular chains: D
Help us to save free conscience from the paw E
Of hireling wolves, whose gospel is their maw. E
stomach

detractions rude: charges brought against Cromwell by Royalists and other opponents.

Darwen: the Battle of Preston, fought near the River Darwen in Lancashire in August 1648.

imbrued: stained.

Dunbar: the Battle of Dunbar, where Cromwell defeated the Scots in September 1650.

Worcester: the Battle of Worcester, where Cromwell defeated Charles II in September 1651.

hireling wolves: disreputable clergy; those who would use the power of the state to enforce conformity to a national church.

maw: stomach, or belly.

A25   John Milton, 'How soon hath Time, the subtle thief of youth'

From D.M. Main (ed.) (1880) *A Treasury of English Sonnets*, Manchester, Alexander Ireland and Co., p.70.

How soon hath Time, the subtle thief of youth,
Stolen on his wing my three-and-twentieth year!
My hasting days fly on with full career,
But my late spring no bud or blossom shew'th.
Perhaps my semblance might deceive the truth
That I to manhood am arrived so near;
And inward ripeness doth much less appear,
That some more timely-happy spirits indu'th.
Yet be it less or more, or soon or slow,
It shall be still in strictest measure even,
To that same lot, however mean or high,
Toward which Time leads me, and the will of Heaven.
All is, if I have grace to use it so,
As ever in my great task-Master's eye.

subtle: cunning.
on his wing: as if in flight.
timely-happy: seasonable.
indu'th: make themselves present.

A26 John Milton, 'Methought I saw my late espousèd saint'

From D.M. Main (ed.) (1880) *A Treasury of English Sonnets*, Manchester, Alexander Ireland and Co., p.77.

Methought I saw my late espousèd saint
Brought to me like Alcestis from the grave,
Whom Jove's great son to her glad husband gave,
Rescued from Death by force, though pale and faint.
Mine, as whom washed from spot of child-bed taint
Purification in the Old Law did save,
And such, as yet once more I trust to have
Full sight of her in Heaven without restraint,
Came vested all in white, pure as her mind:
Her face was veiled; yet to my fancied sight
Love, sweetness, goodness, in her person shined
So clear, as in no face with more delight.
But oh! as to embrace me she inclined,
I waked, she fled, and day brought back my night.

late espousèd: married and now dead.

Alcestis, Jove: in classsical myth, Alcestis is brought back from the dead by Heracles, the son of Zeus (or Jove in biblical myth).

Old Law: the Old Testament Law in Leviticus XII, which concerns the 'purification' of women after childbirth.

A27 Anna Seward (1742–1809), 'Sonnet. December Morning'

From R. Lonsdale (ed.) (1989) *Eighteenth Century Women Poets: An Oxford Anthology*, Oxford, Oxford University Press, pp.315–16.

I love to rise ere gleams the tardy light,
    Winter's pale dawn; – and as warm fires illume,
    And cheerful tapers shine around the room,
    Through misty windows bend my musing sight
Where, round the dusky lawn, the mansions white,
    With shutters closed, peer faintly through the gloom,
    That slow recedes; while yon grey spires assume,
    Rising from their dark pile, an added height
By indistinctness given. – Then to decree
    The grateful thoughts to God, ere they unfold
    To Friendship, or the Muse, or seek with glee
Wisdom's rich page! – O, hours! more worth than gold,
    By whose blest use we lengthen life, and, free
    From drear decays of age, outlive the old!

tardy: unpunctual.

A28 Anna Seward, 'Sonnet. To the Poppy'

From R. Lonsdale (ed.) (1989) *Eighteenth Century Women Poets: An Oxford Anthology*, Oxford, Oxford University Press, p.318.

While summer roses all their glory yield
    To crown the votary of love and joy,
    Misfortune's victim hails, with many a sigh,
    Thee, scarlet Poppy of the pathless field,
Gaudy, yet wild and lone; no leaf to shield
    Thy flaccid vest that, as the gale blows high,
    Flaps, and alternate folds around thy head.
    So stands in the long grass a love-crazed maid,
Smiling aghast; while stream to every wind
    Her garish ribbons, smeared with dust and rain;
    But brain-sick visions cheat her tortured mind,
And bring false peace. Thus, lulling grief and pain,
    Kind dreams oblivious from thy juice proceed,
    Thou flimsy, showy, melancholy weed.

votary: devoted servant.
aghast: struck with amazement.

A29 Charlotte Smith (1749–1806), 'Sonnet Written at the Close of Spring'

From R. Lonsdale (ed.) (1989) *Eighteenth Century Women Poets: An Oxford Anthology*, Oxford, Oxford University Press, p.367.

The garlands fade that Spring so lately wove,
    Each simple flower, which she had nursed in dew,
Anemonies, that spangled every grove,
    The primrose wan, and harebell mildly blue.
No more shall violets linger in the dell,
    Or purple orchis variegate the plain,
Till Spring again shall call forth every bell,
    And dress with humid hands her wreaths again. –
Ah! poor humanity! so frail, so fair,
    Are the fond visions of thy early day,
Till tyrant passion, and corrosive care,
    Bid all thy fairy colours fade away!
Another May new buds and flowers shall bring;
Ah? why has happiness – no second Spring?

A30 Charlotte Smith, 'Sonnet Written in the Church Yard at Middleton in Sussex'

From R. Lonsdale (ed.) (1989) *Eighteenth Century Women Poets: An Oxford Anthology*, Oxford, Oxford University Press, pp.367–8.

Pressed by the moon, mute arbitress of tides,
    While the loud equinox its power combines,
    The sea no more its swelling surge confines,
But o'er the shrinking land sublimely rides.
The wild blast, rising from the western cave,
    Drives the huge billows from their heaving bed,
    Tears from their grassy tombs the village dead,
And breaks the silent sabbath of the grave!
With shells and sea-weed mingled, on the shore
    Lo! their bones whiten in the frequent wave;
    But vain to them the winds and waters rave;
They hear the warring elements no more:
While I am doomed – by life's long storm oppressed,
To gaze with envy on their gloomy rest.

equinox: the moment when the sun crosses the equator.

A31 William Wordsworth (1770–1850), 'Nuns fret not at their convent's narrow room'

From D.M. Main (ed.) (1880) *A Treasury of English Sonnets*, Manchester, Alexander Ireland and Co., p.92.

Nuns fret not at their convent's narrow room;
And hermits are contented with their cells;
And students with their pensive citadels:
Maids at the wheel, the weaver at his loom,
Sit blithe and happy; bees that soar for bloom,
High as the highest Peak of Furness-fells,
Will murmur by the hour in foxglove bells:
In truth, the prison unto which we doom
Ourselves, no prison is: and hence for me,
In sundry moods, 'twas pastime to be bound
Within the Sonnet's scanty plot of ground;
Pleased if some Souls (for such there needs must be)
Who have felt the weight of too much liberty,
Should find brief solace there, as I have found.

A32 William Wordsworth, 'London, 1802'

From D.M. Main (ed.) (1880) *A Treasury of English Sonnets*, Manchester, Alexander Ireland and Co., p.107.

Milton! thou should'st be living at this hour:
England hath need of thee: she is a fen
Of stagnant waters: altar, sword, and pen,
Fireside, the heroic wealth of hall and bower,
Have forfeited their ancient English dower
Of inward happiness. We are selfish men;
Oh! raise us up, return to us again;
And give us manners, virtue, freedom, power.
Thy soul was like a Star, and dwelt apart:
Thou hadst a voice whose sound was like the sea:
Pure as the naked heavens, majestic, free,
So didst thou travel on life's common way,
In cheerful godliness; and yet thy heart
The lowliest duties on herself did lay.

A33 William Wordsworth, 'Composed upon Westminster Bridge, 3 September, 1802'

From D.M. Main (ed.) (1880) *A Treasury of English Sonnets*, Manchester, Alexander Ireland and Co., p.100.

Earth has not anything to show more fair:
Dull would he be of soul who could pass by
A sight so touching in its majesty:
This City now doth like a garment wear
The beauty of the morning; silent, bare,
Ships, towers, domes, theatres, and temples lie
Open unto the fields and to the sky;
All bright and glittering in the smokeless air.
Never did sun more beautifully steep
In his first splendour, valley, rock, or hill;
Ne'er saw I, never felt, a calm so deep!
The river glideth at his own sweet will:
Dear God! the very houses seem asleep;
And all that mighty heart is lying still!

A34 William Wordsworth, 'Scorn not the Sonnet'

From R. Nye (ed.) (1976) *The Faber Book of Sonnets*, London, Faber and Faber, p.109.

Scorn not the Sonnet; Critic, you have frowned,
Mindless of its just honours: with this key
Shakespeare unlocked his heart; the melody
Of this small lute gave ease to Petrarch's wound;
A thousand times this pipe did Tasso sound;
With it Camoens soothed an exile's grief;
The Sonnet glittered a gay myrtle leaf
Amid the cypress with which Dante crowned
His visionary brow; a glow-worm lamp
It cheered mild Spenser, called from Faery-land
To struggle through dark ways; and when a damp
Fell round the path of Milton, in his hand
The Thing became a trumpet, whence he blew
Soul-animating strains – alas, too few!

Petrarch: Italian scholar and poet (1304–74), one of the earliest sonneteers.

Tasso: Torquato Tasso (1544–95), Italian Renaissance poet.

Camoens: Luis de Camoens (1524?–80), Portugal's national poet.

Dante: Dante Alighieri (1265–1321), Italian writer and philosopher, author of *The Divine Comedy.*

Spenser: Edmund Spenser (1552?–99), English poet, author of *The Faerie Queene.*

Milton: John Milton (1608–74), English poet, author of *Paradise Lost.*

A35 Samuel Taylor Coleridge (1772–1834), 'To the River Otter'

From D.M. Main (ed.) (1880) *A Treasury of English Sonnets*, Manchester, Alexander Ireland and Co., p.121.

Dear native brook! wild streamlet of the West!
How many various-fated years have passed,
What happy, and what mournful hours, since last
I skimmed the smooth thin stone along thy breast,
Numbering its light leaps! Yet so deep imprest
Sink the sweet scenes of childhood, that mine eyes
I never shut amid the sunny ray,
But straight with all their tints thy waters rise,
Thy crossing plank, thy marge with willows gray,
And bedded sand that, veined with various dyes,
Gleamed through thy bright transparence. On my way,
Visions of childhood! oft have ye beguiled
Lone manhood's cares, yet waking fondest sighs:
Ah! that once more I were a careless child.

marge: edge, or margin.

A36 Percy Bysshe Shelley (1792–1822), 'England in 1819'

From P. Negri (ed.) (1994) *Great Sonnets*, New York, Dover Publications Inc., p.33.

An old, mad, blind, despised, and dying King, –
Princes, the dregs of their dull race, who flow
Through public scorn, – mud from a muddy spring, –
Rulers who neither see, nor feel, nor know,
But leech-like to their fainting country cling,
Till they drop, blind in blood, without a blow, –
A people starved and stabbed in the untilled field, –
An army, which liberticide and prey
Makes as a two-edged sword to all who wield, –
Golden and sanguine laws which tempt and slay;
Religion Christless, Godless – a book sealed;
A Senate, – Time's worst statute unrepealed, –
Are graves, from which a glorious Phantom may
Burst, to illumine our tempestuous day.

King: George III was over 80 years old and had been insane for many years; he died in 1820.

Princes: George III had nine notorious sons.

field: St Peter's fields at Manchester, where the Peterloo massacre occurred in 1819.

A37 Percy Bysshe Shelley, 'Ozymandias'

From D.M. Main (ed.) (1880) *A Treasury of English Sonnets*, Manchester, Alexander Ireland and Co., p.138.

I met a traveller from an antique land
Who said: Two vast and trunkless legs of stone
Stand in the desert. Near them, on the sand,
Half sunk, a shattered visage lies, whose frown
And wrinkled lip and sneer of cold command
Tell that its sculptor well those passions read
Which yet survive, stamped on these lifeless things,
The hand that mocked them and the heart that fed;
And on the pedestal these words appear:
'My name is Ozymandias, king of kings:
Look on my works, ye Mighty, and despair!'
Nothing beside remains. Round the decay
Of that colossal wreck, boundless and bare
The lone and level sands stretch far away.

Ozymandias: the Greek name of Rameses II (1304–1237 BCE), thought to be the pharaoh of Egypt who oppressed the captive Hebrews.

A38 John Keats (1795–1821), 'To Sleep'

From D.M. Main (ed.) (1880) *A Treasury of English Sonnets*, Manchester, Alexander Ireland and Co., p.156.

O soft embalmer of the still midnight!
Shutting, with careful fingers and benign,
Our gloom-pleased eyes, embowered from the light,
Enshaded in forgetfulness divine:
O soothest Sleep! if so it please thee, close,
In midst of this thine hymn, my willing eyes,
Or wait the amen, ere thy poppy throws
Around my bed its lulling charities;
Then save me, or the passèd day will shine
Upon my pillow, breeding many woes;
Save me from curious conscience, that still lords
Its strength, for darkness burrowing like a mole;
Turn the key deftly in the oilèd wards,
And seal the hushèd casket of my soul.

A39 John Keats, 'When I have fears that I may cease to be'

From D.M. Main (ed.) (1880) *A Treasury of English Sonnets*, Manchester, Alexander Ireland and Co., p.155.

When I have fears that I may cease to be
Before my pen has gleaned my teeming brain,
Before high-pilèd books, in charact'ry
Hold like rich garners the full-ripened grain;
When I behold, upon the night's starred face,
Huge cloudy symbols of a high romance,
And think that I may never live to trace
Their shadows, with the magic hand of chance;
And when I feel, fair creature of an hour,
That I shall never look upon thee more,
Never have relish in the faery power
Of unreflecting love, – then on the shore
Of the wide world I stand alone, and think
Till love and fame to nothingness do sink.

charact'ry: letters, or characters.

A40 John Keats, 'On First Looking into Chapman's Homer'

From D.M. Main (ed.) (1880) *A Treasury of English Sonnets*, Manchester, Alexander Ireland and Co., p.153.

Much have I travelled in the realms of gold,
And many goodly states and kingdoms seen;
Round many western islands have I been
Which bards in fealty to Apollo hold.
Oft of one wide expanse had I been told
That deep-browed Homer ruled as his demesne:
Yet did I never breathe its pure serene
Till I heard Chapman speak out loud and bold:
Then felt I like some watcher of the skies
When a new planet swims into his ken;
Or like stout Cortez, when with eagle eyes
He stared at the Pacific – and all his men
Looked at each other with a wild surmise –
Silent, upon a peak in Darien.

Chapman: George Chapman (1559–1634), English poet, celebrated for his vivid translation of the work of the Greek epic poet, Homer.

fealty: faith, or allegiance.

Apollo: Greek god of prophecy, music and medicine.

demesne: district, or region.

Cortez: Hernán Cortéz (1485–1547), Spanish conquistador and Pacific explorer.

peak in Darien: a mountain in the Panama region.

A41   John Keats, 'Bright star, would I were stedfast as thou art'

From D.M. Main (ed.) (1880) *A Treasury of English Sonnets*, Manchester, Alexander Ireland and Co., p.158.

Bright star, would I were stedfast as thou art, –
Not in lone splendour hung aloft the night,
And watching, with eternal lids apart,
Like nature's patient sleepless Eremite,
The moving waters at their priestlike task
Of pure ablution round earth's human shores,
Or gazing on the new soft-fallen mask
Of snow upon the mountains and the moors: –
No – yet still stedfast, still unchangeable,
Pillowed upon my fair love's ripening breast,
To feel for ever its soft fall and swell,
Awake for ever in a sweet unrest;
Still, still to hear her tender-taken breath,
And so live ever – or else swoon to death.

Eremite: hermit.

A42 John Clare (1793–1864), 'Winter Fields'

From E. Robinson and G. Summerfield (eds) (1966) *Selected Poems and Prose of John Clare*, Oxford, Oxford University Press, p.159.

O for a pleasant book to cheat the sway
Of winter – where rich mirth with hearty laugh
Listens and rubs his legs on corner seat
For fields are mire and sludge – and badly off
Are those who on their pudgy paths delay
There striding shepherd seeking driest way
Fearing nights wetshod feet and hacking cough
That keeps him waken till the peep of day
Goes shouldering onward and with ready hook
Progs oft to ford the sloughs that nearly meet
Across the lands – croodling and thin to view
His loath dog follows – stops and quakes and looks
For better roads – till whistled to pursue
Then on with frequent jump he hirkles through.

pudgy: full of puddles.
progs: prods.
croodling: shrinking, or huddling, from the cold.
hirkles: in a crouching manner.

A43 John Clare, 'The Vixen'

From E. Robinson and G. Summerfield (eds) (1966) *Selected Poems and Prose of John Clare*, Oxford, Oxford University Press, pp.94–5.

Among the taller wood with ivy hung,
The old fox plays and dances round her young.
She snuffs and barks if any passes by
And swings her tail and turns prepared to fly.
The horseman hurries by, she bolts to see,
And turns agen, from danger never free.
If any stands she runs among the poles
And barks and snaps and drives them in the holes.
The shepherd sees them and the boy goes by
And gets a stick and progs the hole to try.
They get all still and lie in safety sure,
And out again when everything's secure,
And start and snap at blackbirds bouncing by
To fight and catch the great white butterfly.

progs: prods

A44 John Clare, 'England, 1830'

From J.W. and Anne Tibble (eds) (1975) *John Clare. Selected Poems*, London, Everyman's Library, Dent, p.194.

These vague allusions to a country's wrongs,
  Where one says 'Ay' and others answer 'No'
In contradiction from a thousand tongues,
  Till like to prison-cells her freedoms grow
Becobwebbed with these oft-repeated songs
  Of peace and plenty in the midst of woe –
And is it thus they mock her year by year,
  Telling poor truth unto her face she lies,
Declaiming of her wealth with gibe severe,
  So long as taxes drain their wished supplies?
And will these jailers rivet every chain
  Anew, yet loudest in their mockery be,
To damn her into madness with disdain,
  Forging new bonds and bidding her be free?

A45 John Clare, 'Sonnet: I Am'

From E. Robinson and G. Summerfield (eds) (1966) *Selected Poems and Prose of John Clare*, Oxford, Oxford University Press, p.196.

I feel I am, I only know I am
And plod upon the earth as dull and void
Earth's prison chilled my body with its dram
Of dullness, and my soaring thoughts destroyed.
I fled to solitudes from passions dream
But strife persued – I only know I am.
I was a being created in the race
Of men disdaining bounds of place and time –
A spirit that could travel o'er the space
Of earth and heaven – like a thought sublime,
Tracing creation, like my maker, free –
A soul unshackled like eternity,
Spurning earth's vain and soul debasing thrall
But now I only know I am – that's all.

A46 Charles Tennyson Turner (1808–79), 'Letty's Globe'

From R. Nye (ed.) (1976) *The Faber Book of Sonnets*, London, Faber and Faber, p.146.

When Letty had scarce passed her third glad year,
And her young artless words began to flow,
One day we gave the child a coloured sphere
Of the wide earth, that she might mark and know,
By tint and outline, all its sea and land.
She patted all the world; old empires peeped
Between her baby fingers. Her soft hand
Was welcome at all frontiers. How she leaped,
And laughed, and prattled, in her world-wide bliss.
But when we turned her sweet unlearned eye
On our own isle, she raised a joyous cry,
'Oh! yes, I see it. Letty's home is there!'
And while she hid all England with a kiss,
Bright over Europe fell her golden hair.

A47   Elizabeth Barrett Browning (1809–61), 'If thou must love me, let it be for nought'

Sonnet XIV of *Sonnets from the Portuguese*, from Shaakeh S. Agajanian (1985) *'Sonnets from the Portuguese' and the Love Sonnet Tradition*, New York, Philosophical Library, p.38.

If thou must love me, let it be for nought
Except for love's sake only. Do not say
'I love her for her smile – her look – her way
Of speaking gently, – for a trick of thought
That falls in well with mine, and certes brought
A sense of pleasant ease on such a day' –
For these things in themselves, Beloved, may
Be changed, or change for thee, – and love, so wrought,
May be unwrought so. Neither love me for
Thine own dear pity's wiping my cheeks dry, –
A creature might forget to weep, who bore
Thy comfort long, and lose thy love thereby!
But love me for love's sake, that evermore
Thou mayst love on, through love's eternity.

A48 Elizabeth Barrett Browning, 'Beloved, thou has brought me many flowers'

Sonnet XLIV of *Sonnets from the Portuguese*, from Shaakeh S. Agajanian (1985) *'Sonnets from the Portuguese' and the Love Sonnet Tradition*, New York, Philosophical Library, p.68.

Beloved, thou has brought me many flowers
Plucked in the garden, all the summer through
And winter, and it seemed as if they grew
In this close room, nor missed the sun and showers
So, in the like name of that love of ours,
Take back these thoughts which here unfolded too,
And which on warm and cold days I withdrew
From my heart's ground. Indeed, those beds and bowers
Be overgrown with bitter weeds and rue,
And wait thy weeding; yet here's eglantine,
Here's ivy! – take them, as I used to do
Thy flowers, and keep them where they shall not pine.
Instruct thine eyes to keep their colours true,
And tell thy soul their roots are left in mine.

A49 George Meredith (1828–1909), 'By this he knew she wept with waking eyes'

Sonnet I in George Meredith, *Modern Love*, S. Regan (ed.), Peterborough, Daisy Books, 1988, p.29.

By this he knew she wept with waking eyes:
That, at his hand's light quiver by her head,
The strange low sobs that shook their common bed,
Were called into her with a sharp surprise,
And strangled mute, like little gaping snakes,
Dreadfully venomous to him. She lay
Stone-still, and the long darkness flowed away
With muffled pulses. Then, as midnight makes
Her giant heart of Memory and Tears
Drink the pale drug of silence, and so beat
Sleep's heavy measure, they from head to feet
Were moveless, looking through their dead black years,
By vain regret scrawled over the blank wall.
Like sculptured effigies they might be seen
Upon their marriage-tomb, the sword between;
Each wishing for the sword that severs all.

A50 George Meredith, 'We saw the swallows gathering in the sky'

Sonnet XLVII in George Meredith, *Modern Love*, S. Regan (ed.), Peterborough, Daisy Books, 1988, p.52.

We saw the swallows gathering in the sky,
And in the osier-isle we heard them noise.
We had not to look back on summer joys,
Or forward to a summer of bright dye:
But in the largeness of the evening earth
Our spirits grew as we went side by side.
The hour became her husband and my bride.
Love that had robbed us so, thus blessed our dearth!
The pilgrims of the year waxed very loud
In multitudinous chatterings, as the flood
Full brown came from the West, and like pale blood
Expanded to the upper crimson cloud.
Love that had robbed us of immortal things,
This little moment mercifully gave,
Where I have seen across the twilight wave
The swan sail with her young beneath her wings.

osier-isle: island of willows.

A51 George Meredith, 'Thus piteously Love closed what he begat'

Sonnet L in George Meredith, *Modern Love*, S. Regan (ed.), Peterborough, Daisy Books, 1988, p.54.

Thus piteously Love closed what he begat:
The union of this ever-diverse pair!
These two were rapid falcons in a snare,
Condemned to do the flitting of the bat.
Lovers beneath the singing sky of May,
They wandered once; clear as the dew on flowers:
But they fed not on the advancing hours:
Their hearts held cravings for the buried day.
Then each applied to each that fatal knife,
Deep questioning, which probes to endless dole.
Ah, what a dusty answer gets the soul
When hot for certainties in this our life! –
In tragic hints here see what evermore
Moves dark as yonder midnight ocean's force,
Thundering like ramping hosts of warrior horse,
To throw that faint thin line upon the shore!

dole: grief.

A52 Dante Gabriel Rossetti (1828–82), Introductory Sonnet to *The House of Life*

From R. Nye (ed.) (1976) *The Faber Book of Sonnets*, London, Faber and Faber, p.160.

A Sonnet is a moment's monument, –
Memorial from the Soul's eternity
To one dead deathless hour. Look that it be,
Whether for lustral rite or dire portent,
Or its own arduous fullness reverent:
Carve it in ivory or in ebony
As Day or Night shall rule; and let Time see
Its flowering crest impearled and orient.
A sonnet is a coin: its face reveals
The soul, – its converse, to what Power 'tis due: –
Whether for tribute to the august appeals
Of Life, or dower in Love's high retinue
It serve, or, mid the dark wharf's cavernous breath,
In Charon's palm it pay the toll to Death.

Charon: in Greek mythology, the ferry man who carries the spirits of the dead across the River Styx.

A53 Dante Gabriel Rossetti, 'Nuptial Sleep'

From C. Ricks (ed.) (1987) *The New Oxford Book of Victorian Verse*, Oxford, Oxford University Press, p.276.

At length their long kiss severed, with sweet smart:
    And as the last slow sudden drops are shed
    From sparkling eaves when all the storm has fled,
So singly flagged the pulses of each heart.
Their bosoms sundered, with the opening start
    Of married flowers to either side outspread
    From the knit stem; yet still their mouths, burnt red,
Fawned on each other where they lay apart.

Sleep sank them lower than the tide of dreams,
    And their dreams watched them sink, and slid away.
Slowly their souls swam up again, through gleams
    Of watered light and dull drowned waifs of day;
Till from some wonder of new woods and streams
    He woke, and wondered more: for there she lay.

A54 Christina Rossetti (1830–94), 'Come back to me, who wait and watch for you'

Sonnet 1 from 'Monna Innominata', in R.W. Crump (ed.) (1986) *The Complete Poems of Christina Rossetti*, Baton Rouge, Louisiana State University Press, vol. II, p.86.

'Lo dì che han detto a' dolci amici addio.' – Dante.
'Amor, con quanto sforzo oggi mi vinci!' – Petrarca.

Come back to me, who wait and watch for you: –
    Or come not yet, for it is over then,
    And long it is before you come again,
So far between my pleasures are and few.
While, when you come not, what I do I do
    Thinking 'Now when he comes,' my sweetest 'when:'
    For one man is my world of all the men
This wide world holds; O love, my world is you.
Howbeit, to meet you grows almost a pang
    Because the pang of parting comes so soon;
My hope hangs waning, waxing, like a moon
    Between the heavenly days on which we meet:
Ah me, but where are now the songs I sang
    When life was sweet because you called them sweet?

Dante quotation: 'The day that they have said adieu to their sweet friends.'
Petrarch quotation: 'Love, with what great force you overthrow me now.'

A55 Christina Rossetti, 'Youth gone, and beauty gone'

Sonnet 14 of 'Monna Innominata' in R.W. Crump (ed.) (1986) *The Complete Poems of Christina Rossetti*, Baton Rouge, Louisiana State University Press, vol. II, p.93.

'E la Sua Volontade è nostra pace.' – Dante.
'Sol con questi pensier, con altre chiome.' – Petrarca.

Youth gone, and beauty gone if ever there
    Dwelt beauty in so poor a face as this;
    Youth gone and beauty, what remains of bliss?
I will not bind fresh roses in my hair,
To shame a cheek at best but little fair, –
    Leave youth his roses, who can bear a thorn, –
I will not seek for blossoms anywhere,
    Except such common flowers as blow with corn.
Youth gone and beauty gone, what doth remain?
    The longing of a heart pent up forlorn,
      A silent heart whose silence loves and longs:
      The silence of a heart which sang its songs
    While youth and beauty made a summer morn,
Silence of love that cannot sing again.

Dante quotation: 'And His will is our peace.'
Petrarch quotation: 'Alone with these my thoughts, with different hair.'

A56 Christina Rossetti, 'Remember'

From R. Nye (ed.) (1976) *The Faber Book of Sonnets*, London, Faber and Faber, p.165.

Remember me when I am gone away,
   Gone far away into the silent land;
   When you can no more hold me by the hand,
Nor I half turn to go yet turning stay.
Remember me when no more day by day
   You tell me of our future that you planned:
   Only remember me; you understand
It will be late to counsel then or pray.
Yet if you should forget me for a while
   And afterwards remember, do not grieve:
   For if the darkness and corruption leave
   A vestige of the thoughts that once I had,
Better by far you should forget and smile
   Than that you should remember and be sad.

A57 Thomas Hardy (1840–1928), 'A Church Romance'

From *The Collected Poems of Thomas Hardy*, London, Macmillan, 1965, p.236.

She turned in the high pew, until her sight
Swept the west gallery, and caught its row
Of music-men with viol, book, and bow
Against the sinking sad tower-window light.

She turned again; and in her pride's despite
One strenuous viol's inspirer seemed to throw
A message from his string to her below,
Which said: 'I claim thee as my own forthright!'

Thus their hearts' bond began, in due time signed.
And long years thence, when Age had scared Romance,
At some old attitude of his or glance
That gallery-scene would break upon her mind,
With him as minstrel, ardent, young, and trim,
Bowing 'New Sabbath' or 'Mount Ephraim.'

'New Sabbath' and 'Mount Ephraim': popular hymns.

A58 Thomas Hardy, 'Hap'

From *The Collected Poems of Thomas Hardy*, London, Macmillan, 1965, p.7.

If but some vengeful god would call to me
From up the sky, and laugh: 'Thou suffering thing,
Know that thy sorrow is my ecstasy,
That thy love's loss is my hate's profiting!'

Then would I bear it, clench myself, and die,
Steeled by the sense of ire unmerited;
Half-eased in that a Powerfuller than I
Had willed and meted me the tears I shed.

But not so. How arrives it joy lies slain,
And why unblooms the best hope ever sown?
– Crass Casualty obstructs the sun and rain,
And dicing Time for gladness casts a moan.
These purblind Doomsters had as readily strown
Blisses about my pilgrimage as pain.

hap: chance, or luck.

A59 Gerard Manley Hopkins (1844–89), 'The Windhover'

From P. Milward (1969) *A Commentary on the Sonnets of G.M. Hopkins*, Chicago, Loyola University Press, p.34.

I cáught this mórning mórning's mínion, kíng-
   dom of dáylight's dáuphin, dapple-dáwn-drawn Fálcon in his riding
   Of the rólling level úndernéath him steady áir, and stríding
Hígh there, how he rúng upon the réin of a wímpling wíng
In his écstasy! then óff, óff fórth on swíng,
   As a skáte's heel sweeps smóoth on a bów-bend: the húrl and glíding
   Rebúffed the bíg wínd. My héart in híding
Stírred for a bírd, – the achíeve of, the mástery of the thíng!

Brute béauty and válour and áct, oh, air, príde, plume, hére
   Búckle! AND the fire that bréaks from thée then, a billion
Tímes told lóvelier, more dángerous, O mý chevalíer!

   No wónder of it: shéer plód makes plóugh down síllion
Shíne, and blúe-bleak émbers, áh my déar,
   Fall, gáll themsélves, and gásh góld-vermílion.

A60 Gerard Manley Hopkins, 'God's Grandeur'

From C. Phillips (ed.) (1986) *Gerard Manley Hopkins*, The Oxford Authors, Oxford University Press, p.4.

The wórld is chárged with the grándeur of Gód.
   It will fláme oút, like shíning from shóok fóil;
   It gáthers to a gréatness, like the óoze of óil
Crushed. Whý do mén then nów not réck his ród?
Génerátions have tród, have tród, have tród;
   And áll is séared with tráde; bleared, sméared with tóil;
   And wéars man's smúdge and sháres man's sméll: the sóil
Is báre now, nór can fóot féel, being shód.

And for áll thís, náture is néver spént;
   There líves the déarest fréshness déep down thíngs;
And thóugh the lást lights óff the bláck West wént
   Oh, mórning, át the brown brink éastward, springs –
Becáuse the Hóly Ghóst óver the bént
   World bróods with wárm breast ánd with áh! bright wíngs.

A61 Gerard Manley Hopkins, 'No worst, there is none'

From C. Phillips (ed.) (1986) *Gerard Manley Hopkins*, The Oxford Authors, Oxford University Press, p.146.

Nó worst, there ís none. Pítched past pítch of gríef,
Móre pangs will, schóoled at fórepangs, wílder wríng.
Cómforter, whére, whére is your cómforting?
Máry, móther of ús, whére is your relíef?
My críes heave, hérds-long; húddle in a máin, a chief-
woe, wórld-sorrow; on an áge-old ánvil wínce and síng –
Then lúll, then léave off. Fúry had shríeked 'No líng-
ering! Lét me be féll: fórce I múst be bríef'.
O the mínd, mínd has móuntains; cliffs of fáll
Fríghtful, sheer, nó-man-fáthomed. Hóld them chéap
Máy who ne'er húng there. Nór does lóng our smáll
Dúrance déal with that stéep or déep. Here! créep,
Wretch, únder a cómfort sérves in a whírlwind: áll
Life déath does énd and éach day díes with sléep.

A62 Gerard Manley Hopkins, 'I wake and feel the fell of dark'

From C. Phillips (ed.) (1986) *Gerard Manley Hopkins*, The Oxford Authors, Oxford University Press, p.158.

I wáke and féel the féll of dárk, not dáy.
What hóurs, O whát black hóürs wé have spént
This níght! what sights you, héart, saw; wáys you wént!
And móre must, ín yet lónger líght's deláy.

With wítness I spéak this. But whére I sáy
Hóurs I mean yéars, mean lífe. And my lamént
Is críes cóuntless, críes like dead létters sént
To déarest him that líves alás! awáy.

I am gáll, I am héartburn. Gód's most déep decrée
Bítter would háve me táste: my táste was mé;
Bones búilt in mé, flesh fílled, blood brímmed the cúrse.

Selfyéast of spírit a dúll dough sóurs. I sée
The lóst are like thís, and théir scóurge to bé
As Í am míne, their swéating sélves; but wórse.

A63 William Butler Yeats (1865–1939), 'Leda and the Swan'

From P. Negri (ed.) (1994) *Great Sonnets*, New York, Dover Publications Inc., p.76.

A sudden blow: the great wings beating still
Above the staggering girl, her thighs caressed
By the dark webs, her nape caught in his bill,
He holds her helpless breast upon his breast.

How can those terrified vague fingers push
The feathered glory from her loosening thighs?
And how can body, laid in that white rush,
But feel the strange heart beating where it lies?

A shudder in the loins engenders there
The broken wall, the burning roof and tower
And Agamemnon dead.
                              Being so caught up,
So mastered by the brute blood of the air,
Did she put on his knowledge with his power
Before the indifferent beak could let her drop?

Leda: in Greek mythology Leda was raped by Zeus (in the form of a swan) and gave birth to Helen of Troy.

Agamemnon: in Greek mythology Agamemnon organized the expedition against Troy for the sake of his brother, Menelaus, whose wife, Helen, had been carried off by Paris.

A64 Rupert Brooke (1887–1915), 'The Soldier'

From P. Negri (ed.) (1994) *Great Sonnets*, New York, Dover Publications Inc., p.83.

If I should die, think only this of me:
   That there's some corner of a foreign field
That is for ever England. There shall be
   In that rich earth a richer dust concealed;
A dust whom England bore, shaped, made aware,
   Gave, once, her flowers to love, her ways to roam,
A body of England's, breathing English air,
   Washed by the rivers, blest by suns of home.

And think, this heart, all evil shed away,
   A pulse in the eternal mind, no less
      Gives somewhere back the thoughts by England given;
Her sights and sounds; dreams happy as her day;
   And laughter, learnt of friends; and gentleness,
      In hearts at peace, under an English heaven.

A65 Claude McKay (1889–1948), 'The White House'

From P. Burnett (ed.) (1986) *The Penguin Book of Caribbean Verse in English*, Harmondsworth, Penguin Books, p.144.

Your door is shut against my tightened face,
And I am sharp as steel with discontent;
But I possess the courage and the grace
To bear my anger proudly and unbent.
The pavement slabs burn loose beneath my feet,
A chafing savage, down the decent street;
And passion rends my vitals as I pass,
Where boldly shines your shuttered door of glass.
Oh, I must search for wisdom every hour,
Deep in my wrathful bosom sore and raw,
And find in it the superhuman power
To hold me to the letter of your law!
Oh, I must keep my heart inviolate
Against the potent poison of your hate.

A66 Claude McKay, 'If we must die'

From P. Burnett (ed.) (1986) *The Penguin Book of Caribbean Verse in English*, Harmondsworth, Penguin Books, p.144.

If we must die, let it not be like hogs
Hunted and penned in an inglorious spot,
While round us bark the mad and hungry dogs,
Making their mock at our accursed lot.
If we must die, O let us nobly die,
So that our precious blood may not be shed
In vain; then even the monsters we defy
Shall be constrained to honour us though dead!
O kinsmen! we must meet the common foe!
Though far outnumbered let us show us brave,
And for their thousand blows deal one deathblow!
What though before us lies the open grave?
Like men we'll face the murderous, cowardly pack,
Pressed to the wall, dying, but fighting back!

A67 Edna St Vincent Millay (1892–1950), 'What lips my lips have kissed, and where, and why'

From P. Negri (ed.) (1994) *Great Sonnets*, New York, Dover Publications Inc., p.85.

What lips my lips have kissed, and where, and why,
I have forgotten, and what arms have lain
Under my head till morning; but the rain
Is full of ghosts tonight, that tap and sigh
Upon the glass and listen for reply,
And in my heart there stirs a quiet pain
For unremembered lads that not again
Will turn to me at midnight with a cry.
Thus in the winter stands the lonely tree,
Nor knows what birds have vanished one by one,
Yet knows its boughs more silent than before:
I cannot say what loves have come and gone,
I only know that summer sang in me
A little while, that in me sings no more.

A68 Wilfred Owen (1893–1918), 'Anthem for Doomed Youth'

From C. Day Lewis (ed.) (1974) *The Collected Poems of Wilfred Owen*, London, Chatto and Windus, pp.178–9.

What passing-bells for these who die as cattle?
   – Only the monstrous anger of the guns.
   Only the stuttering rifles' rapid rattle
Can patter out their hasty orisons.

No mockeries now for them; no prayers nor bells;
   Nor any voice of mourning save the choirs, –
The shrill, demented choirs of wailing shells;
   And bugles calling for them from sad shires.

What candles may be held to speed them all?
   Not in the hands of boys, but in their eyes
Shall shine the holy glimmers of goodbyes.
   The pallor of girls' brows shall be their pall;
Their flowers the tenderness of patient minds,
And each slow dusk a drawing-down of blinds.

A69 Wilfred Owen, 'Hospital Barge at Cérisy'

From E. Blunden (ed.) (1966) *The Poems of Wilfred Owen*, London, Chatto and Windus, p.93.

Budging the sluggard ripples of the Somme,
A barge round old Cérisy slowly slewed.
Softly her engines down the current screwed
And chuckled in her, with contented hum.
Till fairy tinklings struck their crooning dumb.
The waters rumpling at the stern subdued.
The lock-gate took her bulging amplitude.
Gently into the gurgling lock she swum.

One reading by that sunset raised his eyes
To watch her lessening westward quietly,
Till, as she neared the bend, her funnel screamed.
And that long lamentation made him wise
How unto Avalon in agony
Kings passed in the dark barge which Merlin dreamed.

8 December, 1917

A70   Charles Hamilton Sorley (1895–1915), 'When you see millions of the mouthless dead'

From J. Silkin (ed.) (1979) *The Penguin Book of First World War Poetry*, Harmondsworth, Penguin, pp.85–6.

When you see millions of the mouthless dead
Across your dreams in pale battalions go,
Say not soft things as other men have said,
That you'll remember. For you need not so.
Give them not praise. For, deaf, how should they know
It is not curses heaped on each gashed head?
Nor tears. Their blind eyes see not your tears flow.
Nor honour. It is easy to be dead.
Say only this, 'They are dead.' Then add thereto,
'Yet many a better one has died before.'
Then, scanning all the o'ercrowded mass, should you
Perceive one face that you loved heretofore,
It is a spook. None wears the face you knew.
Great death has made all his for evermore.

A71 Edmund Blunden (1896–1974), 'Vlamertinghe: Passing the Château, July, 1917'

From J. Silkin (ed.) (1979) *The Penguin Book of First World War Poetry*, Harmondsworth, Penguin, p.102.

'And all her silken flanks with garlands drest' –
But we are coming to the sacrifice.
Must those have flowers who are not yet gone West?
May those have flowers who live with death and lice?
This must be the floweriest place
That earth allows; the queenly face
Of the proud mansion borrows grace for grace
Spite of those brute guns lowing at the skies.

Bold great daisies' golden lights,
Bubbling roses' pinks and whites –
Such a gay carpet! poppies by the million;
Such damask! such vermilion!
But if you ask me, mate, the choice of colour
Is scarcely right; this red should have been duller.

'And all her silken flanks...': a quotation from 'Ode on a Grecian Urn' by John Keats; stanza IV of the poem begins 'Who are these coming to the sacrifice?'

not yet gone West: not yet killed.

A72   Dylan Thomas (1914–53), 'Altarwise by owl-light in the half-way house'

Sonnet I of *Altarwise by Owl-Light*, in Dylan Thomas (1966) *The Collected Poems 1934–1952*, London, Dent, p.65.

Altarwise by owl-light in the half-way house
The gentleman lay graveward with his furies;
Abaddon in the hangnail cracked from Adam,
And, from his fork, a dog among the fairies,
The atlas-eater with a jew for news,
Bit out the mandrake with to-morrow's scream.
Then, penny-eyed, that gentleman of wounds,
Old cock from nowheres and the heaven's egg,
With bones unbuttoned to the half-way winds,
Hatched from the windy salvage on one leg,
Scraped at my cradle in a walking word
That night of time under the Christward shelter:
I am the long world's gentleman, he said,
And share my bed with Capricorn and Cancer.

Abaddon: in the Old Testament (Job), Abaddon is a figure of death and destruction; in the New Testament (Revelation), Abaddon is a fallen angel.

A73 Dylan Thomas, 'Let the tale's sailor from a Christian voyage'

Sonnet X of *Altarwise by Owl-Light*, in Dylan Thomas (1966) *The Collected Poems 1934–1952*, London, Dent, p.69.

Let the tale's sailor from a Christian voyage
Atlaswise hold half-way off the dummy bay
Time's ship-racked gospel on the globe I balance:
So shall winged harbours through the rockbirds' eyes
Spot the blown word, and on the seas I image
December's thorn screwed in a brow of holly.
Let the first Peter from a rainbow's quayrail
Ask the tall fish swept from the bible east,
What rhubarb man peeled in her foam-blue channel
Has sown a flying garden round that sea-ghost?
Green as beginning, let the garden diving
Soar, with its two bark towers, to that Day
When the worm builds with the gold straws of venom
My nest of mercies in the rude, red tree.

A74 Gwendolyn Brooks (b.1917) 'First fight. Then fiddle'

From Gwendolyn Brooks (1944) *Selected Poems*, Harper and Row, p.54.

First fight. Then fiddle. Ply the slipping string
With feathery sorcery; muzzle the note
With hurting love; the music that they wrote
Bewitch, bewilder. Qualify to sing
Threadwise. Devise no salt, no hempen thing
For the dear instrument to bear. Devote
The bow to silks and honey. Be remote
A while from malice and from murdering.
But first to arms, to armor. Carry hate
In front of you and harmony behind.
Be deaf to music and to beauty blind.
Win war. Rise bloody, maybe not too late
For having first to civilize a space
Wherein to play your violin with grace.

A75   Gwendolyn Brooks, 'What shall I give my children?'

From Gwendolyn Brooks (1944) *Selected Poems*, Harper and Row, p.53.

What shall I give my children? who are poor,
Who are adjudged the leastwise of the land,
Who are my sweetest lepers, who demand
No velvet and no velvety velour;
But who have begged me for a brisk contour,
Crying that they are quasi, contraband
Because unfinished, graven by a hand
Less than angelic, admirable or sure.
My hand is stuffed with mode, design, device.
But I lack access to my proper stone.
And plenitude of plan shall not suffice
Nor grief nor love shall be enough alone
To ratify my little halves who bear
Across an autumn freezing everywhere.

A76   John Gillespie Magee (1922–41), 'High Flight'

From *The Complete Works of John Magee, the Pilot Poet*, Cheltenham, This England Books, 1989, p.79.

Oh! I have slipped the surly bonds of earth
And danced the skies on laughter-silvered wings;
Sunward I've climbed, and joined the tumbling mirth
Of sun-split clouds and done a hundred things
You have not dreamed of – wheeled and soared and swung
High in the sunlit silence. Hov'ring there,
I've chased the shouting wind along, and flung
My eager craft through footless halls of air.
Up, up the long, delirious burning blue
I've topped the wind-swept heights with easy grace
Where never Lark, or even Eagle flew –
And while with silent lifting mind I've trod
The high untrespassed sanctity of space,
Put out my hand and touched the face of God.

A77 Derek Walcott (b.1930), Chapters III, VI and X of 'Tales of the Islands'

From Derek Walcott (1986) *Collected Poems 1948–1984*, New York, The Noonday Press, Farrar, Straus and Giroux, pp.23–5, 27.

Chapter III/ La belle qui fut ...

Miss Rossignol lived in the lazaretto
For Roman Catholic crones; she had white skin,
And underneath it, fine, old-fashioned bones;
She flew like bats to vespers every twilight,
The living Magdalen of Donatello;
And tipsy as a bottle when she stalked
On stilted legs to fetch the morning milk,
In a black shawl harnessed by rusty brooches.
My mother warned us how that flesh knew silk
Coursing a green estate in gilded coaches.
While Miss Rossignol, in the cathedral loft,
Sang to her one dead child, a tattered saint
Whose pride had paupered beauty to this witch
Who was so fine once, whose hands were so soft.

Chapter VI

Poopa, da' was a fête! I mean it had
Free rum free whisky and some fellars beating
Pan from one of them band in Trinidad,
And everywhere you turn was people eating
And drinking and don't name me but I think
They catch his wife with two tests up the beach
While he drunk quoting Shelley with 'Each
Generation has its angst, but we has none'
And wouldn't let a comma in edgewise.
(Black writer chap, one of them Oxbridge guys.)
And it was round this part once that the heart
Of a young child was torn from it alive
By two practitioners of native art,
But that was long before this jump and jive.

Chapter X/ 'Adieu foulard ...'

I watched the island narrowing the fine
Writing of foam around the precipices, then
The roads as small and casual as twine
Thrown on its mountains; I watched till the plane
Turned to the final north and turned above
The open channel with the grey sea between
The fishermen's islets until all that I love
Folded in cloud; I watched the shallow green
That broke in places where there would be reef,
The silver glinting on the fuselage, each mile
Dividing us and all fidelity strained
Till space would snap it. Then, after a while
I thought of nothing; nothing, I prayed, would change;
When we set down at Seawell it had rained.

lazaretto: hospital for the diseased poor, especially lepers.
Donatello: Italian Renaissance sculptor (1386–1466).
pan: steelpan (band instrument).
tests: fellows.

A78 R.S. Thomas (b.1913), 'Composition'

From R.S. Thomas (1967) *Poetry for Supper*, London, Rupert Hart-Davis, p.40.

He never could decide what to write
About, knowing only that his pen
Must not rust in the stale tears of men
Too long dead, nor yet take to flight
Before measuring the thought's height
Above the earth, whose green thoroughfares,
Though hedged thickly with the heart's cares,
Still let in the sun's natural light.

He tried truth; but the pen's scalpel tip
Was too sharp; thinly the blood ran
From unseen wounds, but too red to dip
Again in, so, back where he began,
He tried love; slowly the blood congealed
Like dark flowers saddening a field.

A79 Edwin Morgan (b.1920), 'A mean wind wanders through the backcourt trash'

Sonnet i from *Glasgow Sonnets* in Edwin Morgan (1982) *Poems of Thirty Years*, Manchester, Carcanet New Press, p.283.

A mean wind wanders through the backcourt trash.
Hackles on puddles rise, old mattresses
puff briefly and subside. Play-fortresses
of brick and bric-a-brac spill out some ash.
Four storeys have no windows left to smash,
but in the fifth a chipped sill buttresses
mother and daughter the last mistresses
of that black block condemned to stand, not crash.
Around them the cracks deepen, the rats crawl.
The kettle whimpers on a crazy hob.
Roses of mould grow from ceiling to wall.
The man lies late since he has lost his job,
smokes on one elbow, letting his cough fall
thinly into an air too poor to rob.

A80 Edwin Morgan, 'See a tenement due for demolition'

Sonnet iii from *Glasgow Sonnets* in Edwin Morgan (1982) *Poems of Thirty Years*, Manchester, Carcanet New Press, pp.283–4.

'See a tenement due for demolition?
I can get ye rooms in it, two, okay?
Seven hundred and nothin legal to pay
for it's no legal, see? That's my proposition,
ye can take it or leave it but. The position
is simple, you want a hoose, I say
for eight hundred pounds it's yours.' And they,
trailing five bairns, accepted his omission
of the foul crumbling stairwell, windows wired
not glazed, the damp from the canal, the cooker
without pipes, packs of rats that never tired –
any more than the vandals bored with snooker
who stripped the neighbouring houses, howled, and fired
their aerosols – of squeaking 'Filthy lucre!'

A81 Douglas Dunn (b.1942), 'A Silver Air Force'

From Douglas Dunn (1985) *Elegies*, London, Faber and Faber, p.18.

They used to spin in the light, monoplanes,
Biplanes, a frivolous deterrent to
What had to happen. Silver-winged campaigns,
Dogfights against death, she blew, and I blew,
The mobile spun: Faith, Hope and Charity,
Wing and a Prayer, shot down, shot down in flames.
I watched, and thought, 'What will become of me
When she is dead?' I scramble in my dreams
Again, and see these secret Spitfires fly
As the inevitable aces of the sky,
Hanging from threads, a gentle violence.
But day by day they fell, and each plane crashed
On far, hereafter wheatfields in God's distance –
White strings of hope a summer blueness washed.

A82 Douglas Dunn, 'The Kaleidoscope'

From Douglas Dunn (1986) *Selected Poems 1964–1983*, London, Faber and Faber, p.238.

To climb these stairs again, bearing a tray,
Might be to find you pillowed with your books,
Your inventories listing gowns and frocks
As if preparing for a holiday.
Or, turning from the landing, I might find
My presence watched through your kaleidoscope,
A symmetry of husbands, each redesigned
In lovely forms of foresight, prayer and hope.
I climb these stairs a dozen times a day
And, by that open door, wait, looking in
At where you died. My hands become a tray
Offering me, my flesh, my soul, my skin.
Grief wrongs us so. I stand, and wait, and cry
For the absurd forgiveness, not knowing why.

A83 Douglas Dunn, 'Sandra's Mobile'

From Douglas Dunn (1986) *Selected Poems 1964–1983*, London, Faber and
Faber, p.239.

A constant artist, dedicated to
Curves, shapes, the pleasant shades, the feel of colour,
She did not care what shapes, what red, what blue,
Scorning the dull to ridicule the duller
With a disinterested, loyal eye.
So Sandra brought her this and taped it up –
Three seagulls from a white and indoor sky –
A gift of old artistic comradeship.
'Blow on them, Love.' Those silent birds winged round
On thermals of my breath. On her last night,
Trying to stay awake, I saw love crowned
In tears and wooden birds and candlelight.
She did not wake again. To prove our love
Each gull, each gull, each gull, turned into dove.

A84 Tony Harrison (b.1937), 'On Not Being Milton'

From Tony Harrison (1981) *Continuous. 50 Sonnets from the School of Eloquence*, London, Rex Collings, no page number.

for Sergio Vieira & Armando Guebuza (Frelimo)

Read and committed to the flames, I call
these sixteen lines that go back to my roots
my *Cahier d'un retour au pays natal,*
my growing black enough to fit my boots.

The stutter of the scold out of the branks
of condescension, class and counter-class
thickens with glottals to a lumpen mass
of Ludding morphemes closing up their ranks.
Each swung cast-iron Enoch of Leeds stress
clangs a forged music on the frames of Art,
the looms of owned language smashed apart!

Three cheers for mute ingloriousness!

Articulation is the tongue-tied's fighting.
In the silence round all poetry we quote
Tidd the Cato Street conspirator who wrote:

Sir, I Ham a very Bad Hand at Righting.

Note [by Harrison]: An 'Enoch' is an iron sledge-hammer used by the Luddites to smash the frames which were also made by the same Enoch Taylor of Marsden. The cry was: Enoch made them, Enoch shall break them!

Cahier d'un retour au pays natal: Return to the country of my birth, the title of a sequence of poems by the black Martinique poet, Aimé Césaire (b.1913).

branks: a metal instrument designed to cover the tongue and inhibit speech.

Tidd: one of the political radicals who planned to assassinate members of the cabinet and seize power in 1820. They were arrested in Cato Street in London.

A85 Tony Harrison, 'Them & [uz]'

From Tony Harrison (1981) *Continuous. 50 Sonnets from The School of Eloquence*, London, Rex Collings, no page number.

for Professors Richard Hoggart & Leon Cortez

I

aiaĩ ay, ay! ... stutterer Demosthenes
gob full of pebbles outshouting seas –

4 words only of *mi 'art aches* and ... 'Mine's broken,
you barbarian, T.W.!' *He* was nicely spoken.
'Can't have our glorious heritage done to death!'

I played the Drunken Porter in *Macbeth*.

'Poetry's the speech of kings. You're one of those
Shakespeare gives the comic bits to: prose!
All poetry (even Cockney Keats?) you see
's been dubbed by [Λs] into RP,
Received Pronunciation, please believe [Λs]
your speech is in the hands of the Receivers.'

'We say [Λs] not [uz] T.W.!' That shut my trap.
I doffed my flat a's (as in 'flat cap')
my mouth all stuffed with glottals, great
lumps to hawk up and spit out ... *E-nun-ci-ate*!

II

So right, yer buggers, then! We'll occupy
your lousy leasehold Poetry.

I chewed up Littererchewer and spat the bones
into the lap of dozing Daniel Jones,
dropped the initials I'd been harried as
and used my *name* and own voice: [uz] [uz] [uz],
ended sentences with by, with, from,
and spoke the language that I spoke at home.
R.I.P. RP, R.I.P. T.W.
I'm *Tony* Harrison no longer you!

You can tell the Receivers where to go
(and not aspirate it) once you know
Wordsworth's *matter/water* are full rhymes,
[uz] can be loving as well as funny.

My first mention in the *Times*
automatically made Tony Anthony!

aiaī ay, ay!: the Greek expression of tragic grief, followed by the colloquial English greeting (often used in popular comedy).

Demosthenes: a renowned Greek orator who overcame his speech impediment by shouting to the waves.

mi 'art aches: the opening of 'Ode to a Nightingale' by John Keats.

Daniel Jones: (1881–1967), Professor Emeritus of Phonetics in the University of London and author of several books on the pronunciation of English.

T.W.: the poet's initials.

A86 Tony Harrison, 'Book Ends'

From Tony Harrison (1981) *Continuous. 50 Sonnets from The School of Eloquence*, London, Rex Collings, no page number.

I

Baked the day she suddenly dropped dead
we chew it slowly that last apple pie.

Shocked into sleeplessness you're scared of bed.
We never could talk much, and now don't try.

You're like book ends, the pair of you, she'd say,
Hog that grate, say nothing, sit, sleep, stare ...

The 'scholar' me, you, worn out on poor pay,
only our silence made us seem a pair.

Not as good for staring in, blue gas,
too regular each bud, each yellow spike.

A night you need my company to pass
and she not here to tell us we're alike!

Your life's all shattered into smithereens.

Back in our silences and sullen looks,
for all the Scotch we drink, what's still between's
not the thirty or so years, but books, books, books.

II

Though my mother was already two years dead
Dad kept her slippers warming by the gas,
put hot water bottles her side of the bed
and still went to renew her transport pass.

You couldn't just drop in. You had to phone.
He'd put you off an hour to give him time
to clear away her things and look alone
as though his still raw love were such a crime.

He couldn't risk my blight of disbelief
though sure that very soon he'd hear her key
scrape in the rusted lock and end his grief.
He *knew* she'd just popped out to get the tea.

I believe life ends with death, and that is all.
You haven't both gone shopping; just the same,
in my new black leather phone book there's your name
and the disconnected number I still call.

A87 Tony Harrison, 'Continuous'

From Tony Harrison (1981) *Continuous. 50 Sonnets from The School of Eloquence*, London, Rex Collings, no page number.

James Cagney was the one up both our streets.
His was the only art we ever shared.
A gangster film and choc ice were the treats
that showed about as much love as he dared.

He'd be my own age now in '49!
The hand that glinted with the ring he wore,
his father's, tipped the cold bar into mine
just as the organist dropped through the floor.

He's on the platform lowered out of sight
to organ music, this time on looped tape,
into a furnace with a blinding light
where only his father's ring will keep its shape.

I wear it now to Cagneys on my own
and sense my father's hands cupped round my treat —

they feel as though they've been chilled to the bone
from holding my ice cream all through *White Heat*.

White Heat: a popular Hollywood movie, starring James Cagney.

A88 Seamus Heaney (b.1939), 'Fear of affectation made her affect'

Sonnet 4 from 'Clearances', in Seamus Heaney (1987) *The Haw Lantern*, London, Faber and Faber, p.28.

Fear of affectation made her affect
Inadequacy whenever it came to
Pronouncing words 'beyond her'. *Bertold Brek.*
She'd manage something hampered and askew
Every time, as if she might betray
The hampered and inadequate by too
Well-adjusted a vocabulary.
With more challenge than pride, she'd tell me, 'You
Know all them things.' So I governed my tongue
In front of her, a genuinely well-
adjusted adequate betrayal
Of what I knew better. I'd *naw* and *aye*
And decently relapse into the wrong
Grammar which kept us allied and at bay.

A89 Seamus Heaney, 'The cool that came off sheets just off the line'

Sonnet 5 from 'Clearances', in Seamus Heaney (1987) *The Haw Lantern*, London, Faber and Faber, p.29.

The cool that came off sheets just off the line
Made me think the damp must still be in them
But when I took my corners of the linen
And pulled against her, first straight down the hem
And then diagonally, then flapped and shook
The fabric like a sail in a cross-wind,
They made a dried-out undulating thwack.
So we'd stretch and fold and end up hand to hand
For a split second as if nothing had happened
For nothing had that had not always happened
Beforehand, day by day, just touch and go,
Coming close again by holding back
In moves where I was x and she was o
Inscribed in sheets she'd sewn from ripped-out flour sacks.

A90   Seamus Heaney, 'I thought of walking round and round a space'

Sonnet 8 from 'Clearances', in Seamus Heaney (1987) *The Haw Lantern*, London, Faber and Faber, p.32.

I thought of walking round and round a space
Utterly empty, utterly a source
Where the decked chestnut tree had lost its place
In our front hedge above the wallflowers.
The white chips jumped and jumped and skited high.
I heard the hatchet's diffcrentiated
Accurate cut, the crack, the sigh
And collapse of what luxuriated
Through the shocked tips and wreckage of it all.
Deep planted and long gone, my coeval
Chestnut from a jam jar in a hole,
Its heft and hush become a bright nowhere,
A soul ramifying and forever
Silent, beyond silence listened for.

A91   Wendy Cope (b.1945), 'Faint Praise'

From Wendy Cope (1992) *Serious Concerns*, London, Faber and Faber, p.65.

Size isn't everything. It's what you do
That matters, darling, and you do quite well
In some respects. Credit where credit's due –
You work, you're literate, you rarely smell.
Small men can be aggressive, people say,
But you are often genial and kind,
As long as you can have things all your way
And I comply, and do not speak my mind.
You look all right. I've never been disgusted
By paunchiness. Who wants some skinny youth?
My friends have warned me that you can't be trusted
But I protest I've heard you tell the truth.
Nobody's perfect. Now and then, my pet,
You're almost human. You could make it yet.

A92 Wendy Cope, 'Strugnell's Bargain'

From Headland 'Poetry Live' Card, West Kirkby, Headland Publications, 1987.

My true love hath my heart and I have hers –
We swapped last Tuesday and felt quite elated –
But now whenever one of us refers
To 'my heart' things get rather complicated.
Just now, when she complained 'My heart is racing',
'You mean my heart is racing,' I replied.
'That's what I said.' 'You mean the heart replacing
Your heart, my love.' 'Oh piss off, Jake!' she cried.
I ask you, do you think Sir Philip Sidney
Got spoken to like that? And I suspect
If I threw in my liver and a kidney,
She'd still address me with as scant respect.
Therefore do I revoke my opening line:
My love can keep her heart and I'll have mine.

A93 Wendy Cope, 'The Sitter'

From J. Collins and E. Lindner (eds) (1993) *Writing on the Wall: women writers on women artists*, London, Weidenfeld and Nicolson.

Depressed and disagreeable and fat:
That's how she saw me. It was all she saw.
Around her, yes, I may have looked like that.
She hardly spoke, she thought I was a bore.
Beneath her gaze I couldn't help but slouch.
She made me feel ashamed, my face went red.
I'd rather have been posing on a couch
For some old rake who wanted me in bed.
Some people made me smile, they made me shine,
They made me beautiful, but they're all gone,
Those friends, the way they saw this face of mine.
And her contempt for me is what lives on.
Admired, well-bred, artistic Mrs Bell,
I hope you're looking hideous in hell.

A94 Dana Gioia (b. 1950), 'Sunday Night in Santa Rosa'

From Dana Gioia (1986) *Daily Horoscope. Poems by Dana Gioia*, Saint Paul, Graywolf Press, p.87.

The carnival is over. The high tents,
the palaces of light, are folded flat
and trucked away. A three-time loser yanks
the Wheel of Fortune off the wall. Mice
pick through the garbage by the popcorn stand.
A drunken giant falls asleep beside
the juggler, and the Dog-Faced Boy sneaks off
to join the Serpent Lady for the night.
Wind sweeps ticket stubs along the walk.
The Dead Man loads his coffin on a truck.
Off in a trailer by the parking lot
the radio predicts tomorrow's weather
while a clown stares in a dressing mirror,
takes out a box, and peels away his face.

Section B PHILOSOPHY: REASONING

B1 Bryan Magee, What makes a thinker a philosopher?

From Bryan Magee (1987) *The Great Philosophers*, Oxford, Oxford University Press, p.66.

Any philosopher of any significance must hold at least some beliefs which differentiate him from everyone else, otherwise he would not be significant. Over the millennia almost every imaginable variety of philosophical belief has been held by some philosopher or other. What differentiates a reputable philosopher from disreputable ones is not that there is some 'correct' canonical set of beliefs which he holds but that, whatever his beliefs, he is prepared to put up reasons for them and to see those reasons subjected to scrutiny of the utmost rigour, and to abide by the outcome. He subjects his concepts *and* his arguments *and* his methods to critical analysis, not only on the part of others but on his own part, and lives with the consequences. Provided he does this with full intellectual honesty he can be a Christian or a Hindu or an atheist or anything and be a proper philosopher. Of course, there are some beliefs which have been shown by analysis to be so flawed – incoherent, perhaps, or self-contradictory – that it is now no longer possible, as it might once have been, for someone who is both intelligent and intellectually honest to hold them. The abandonment of such beliefs is part of what constitutes intellectual advance.

B2 What can philosophy contribute to public debate?

From Law Commission Consultation Paper 139 (1995) *Consent in the Criminal Law*, London, HMSO Publications, Appendix C, 'Consent and the criminal law: philosophical foundations', paragraph C4, p.246.

What philosophy can do is to bring to the surface what is already implicit in different arguments or more general positions in a debate. It makes explicit the implications of particular positions and, often just as importantly, it illustrates what those assertions or positions do *not* entail. It demands that any assertion or position should be backed up by arguments, in the form of reasons, for holding the beliefs and commitments which underpin it. And, finally, philosophical investigation can help us to develop criteria for evaluating the arguments that we put forward to substantiate our positions.

B3   Mary Warnock, What is the value of studying philosophy?

From an interview with Mary Warnock for TV4, recorded February 1996.

It's very difficult for me to answer the question what the value of studying philosophy is because I've always enjoyed it so much. I do think that, among other things, it's an exceptionally interesting subject because it relates directly to a lot of things that we take for granted, like the way we talk, what we mean when we say things, and presuppositions that we have that we've never looked at before. [...] It's a wonderful subject to teach and learn because of the involvement of dialogue. Philosophers on the whole don't go off in their studies all by themselves: they tend to like to talk to people, and obviously talking is great fun. So it's an enjoyable subject. But I think, as well, that it probably has some effect in clarifying the way people think: being careful not to use words loosely; thinking 'hang on, what do I actually mean? what am I trying to say? and isn't there a better way of saying it?' Now those sorts of habits are very useful to all kinds of different people who are not philosophers at all.

B4   Nigel Warburton, What is philosophy?

From Nigel Warburton (1995) *Philosophy: The Basics*, London, Routledge, pp.1–6.

What is philosophy? This is a notoriously difficult question. One of the easiest ways of answering it is to say that philosophy is what philosophers do, and then point to the writings of Plato, Aristotle, Descartes, Hume, Kant, Russell, Wittgenstein, Sartre, and other famous philosophers. However, this answer is unlikely to be of much use to you if you are just beginning the subject, as you probably won't have read anything by these writers. Even if you have, it may still be difficult to say what they have in common, if indeed there is a relevant characteristic which they all share. Another approach to the question is to point out that philosophy is derived from the Greek word meaning 'love of wisdom'. However, this is rather vague and even less helpful than saying that philosophy is what philosophers do. So some very general comments about what philosophy is are needed.

Philosophy is an activity: it is a way of thinking about certain sorts of question. Its distinctive feature is its use of logical argument. Philosophers typically deal in arguments: they either invent them, criticize other people's, or do both. They also analyse and clarify concepts. The word 'philosophy' is often used in a much broader sense than this to mean one's general outlook on life, or else to refer to some forms of mysticism. I will not be using the word in this broader sense here: my aim is to illuminate some of the key areas of discussion in a tradition of thought which began with the Ancient Greeks and has flourished in the twentieth century, predominantly in Europe and America.

What kind of things do philosophers working in this tradition argue about? They often examine beliefs that most of us take for granted most of the time. They are concerned with questions about what could loosely be called 'the meaning of life': questions about religion, right and wrong, politics, the nature of the external world, the mind, science, art, and numerous other topics. For instance, most people live their lives without questioning their fundamental beliefs, such as that killing is wrong. But why is it wrong? What justification is there for saying that killing is wrong? Is it wrong in every circumstance? And what do I mean by 'wrong' anyway? These are philosophical questions. Many of our beliefs, when examined, turn out to have firm foundations; but some do not. The study of philosophy not only helps us to think clearly about our prejudices, but also helps to clarify precisely what we do believe. In the process it develops an ability to argue coherently on a wide range of issues – a useful transferable skill.

Philosophy and its history

Since the time of Socrates there have been many great philosophers. I named a few of these in my opening paragraph. An introductory book on philosophy could approach the subject historically, analysing the contributions of these philosophers in chronological order. This is not what I shall do here. Instead I will use a topic-based approach: one focusing on particular philosophical questions rather than on history. The history of philosophy is a fascinating and important subject in its own right, and many of the classic philosophical texts are also great works of literature: Plato's Socratic dialogues, René Descartes' *Meditations*, David Hume's *Enquiry Concerning Human Understanding*, and Friedrich Nietzsche's *Thus Spake Zarathustra*, to take just a few examples, all stand out as compelling pieces of writing by any standards. Whilst there is great value in the study of the history of philosophy, my aim here is to give you the tools to think about philosophical issues yourselves rather than simply to explain what certain great figures have thought about them. These issues are not just of interest to philosophers: they arise naturally out of the human situation and many people who have never opened a philosophy book spontaneously think about them.

Any serious study of philosophy will involve a mixture of historical and topic-based study, since if we don't know about the arguments and errors of earlier philosophers, we cannot hope to make a substantial contribution to the subject. Without some knowledge of history philosophers would never progress: they would keep making the same mistakes, unaware that they had been made before. And many philosophers develop their own theories by seeing what is wrong with the work of earlier philosophers. [...]

Why study philosophy?

It is sometimes argued that there is no point in studying philosophy as all philosophers ever do is sit around quibbling over the meaning of words. They never seem to reach any conclusions of any importance and their contribution to society is virtually non-existent. They are still arguing about the same problems that interested the Ancient Greeks. Philosophy does not seem to change anything; philosophy leaves everything as it is.

What is the value of studying philosophy at all? Starting to question the fundamental assumptions of our lives could even be dangerous: we might end up feeling unable to do anything, paralysed by questioning too much. Indeed, the caricature of a philosopher is of someone who is brilliant at dealing with very abstract thought in the comfort of an armchair in an Oxford or Cambridge common room, but is hopeless at dealing with the practicalities of life: someone who can explain the most complicated passages of Hegel's philosophy, but can't work out how to boil an egg.

The examined life

One important reason for studying philosophy is that it deals with fundamental questions about the meaning of our existence. Most of us at some time in our lives ask ourselves basic philosophical questions. Why are we here? Is there any proof that God exists? Is there any purpose to our lives? What makes anything right or wrong? Could we ever be justified in breaking the law? Could our lives be just a dream? Is mind different from body, or are we simply physical beings? How does science progress? What is art? And so on.

Most people who study philosophy believe that it is important that each of us examines such questions. Some even argue that an unexamined life is not worth living. To carry on a routine existence without ever examining the principles on which it is based may be like driving a car which has never been serviced. You may be justified in trusting the brakes, the steering, the engine, since they have always worked well enough up until now; but you may be completely unjustified in this trust: the brake pads may be faulty and fail you when you most need them. Similarly the principles on which your life is based may be entirely sound, but until you've examined them, you cannot be certain of this.

However, even if you do not seriously doubt the soundness of the assumptions on which your life is based, you may be impoverishing your life by not exercising your power of thought. Many people find it either too much of an effort, or too disturbing to ask themselves such fundamental questions: they may be happy and comfortable with their prejudices. But others have a strong desire to find answers to challenging philosophical questions.

Learning to think

Another reason for studying philosophy is that it provides a good way of learning to think more clearly about a wide range of issues. The methods of philosophical thought can be useful in a wide variety of situations, since by analysing the arguments for and against any position we learn skills which can be transferred to other areas of life. Many people who study philosophy go on to apply their philosophical skills in jobs as diverse as the law, computer programming, management consultancy, the civil service, and journalism – all areas in which clarity of thought is a great asset. Philosophers also use the insights they gain about the nature of human existence when they turn to the arts: a number of philosophers have also been successful as novelists, critics, poets, film-makers and playwrights.

Pleasure

A further justification for the study of philosophy is that for many people it can be a very pleasurable activity. There is something to be said for this defence of philosophy. Its danger is that it could be taken to be reducing philosophical activity to the equivalent of solving crossword puzzles. At times some philosophers' approach to the subject can seem very like this: some professional philosophers become obsessed with solving obscure logical puzzles as an end in itself, publishing their solutions in esoteric journals. At another extreme, some philosophers working in universities see themselves as part of a 'business', and publish what is often mediocre work simply because it will allow them to 'get on' and achieve promotion (quantity of publications being a factor in determining who is promoted). They experience pleasure from seeing their name in print, and from the increased salary and prestige that go with promotion. Fortunately, however, much philosophy rises above this level.

Is philosophy difficult?

Philosophy is often described as a difficult subject. There are various kinds of difficulty associated with it, some avoidable.

In the first place it is true that many of the problems with which professional philosophers deal do require quite a high level of abstract thought. However, the same is true of almost any intellectual pursuit: philosophy is no different in this respect from physics, literary criticism, computer programming, geology, mathematics, or history. As with these and other areas of study, the difficulty of making substantial original contributions to the subject should not be used as an excuse for denying ordinary people knowledge of advances made in it, nor for preventing them learning their basic methods.

However, there is a second kind of difficulty associated with philosophy which can be avoided. Philosophers are not always good writers. Many of them are extremely poor communicators of their ideas. Sometimes this is because they are only interested in reaching a very small audience of specialist readers; sometimes it is because they use unnecessarily complicated jargon which simply confuses those unfamiliar with it. Specialist terms can be helpful to avoid having to explain particular concepts every time they are used. However, among professional philosophers there is an unfortunate tendency to use specialist terms for their own sake; many of them use Latin phrases even though there are perfectly good English equivalents. A paragraph peppered with unfamiliar words and familiar words used in unfamiliar ways can be intimidating. Some philosophers seem to speak and write in a language they have invented themselves. This can make philosophy appear to be a much more difficult subject than it really is. [...]

The limits of what philosophy can do

Some students of philosophy have unreasonably high expectations of the subject. They expect it to provide them with a complete and detailed picture of the human predicament. They think that philosophy will reveal to them the meaning of life, and explain to them every facet of our complex existences. Now, although studying philosophy can illuminate fundamental questions about our lives, it does not provide anything like a complete picture, if indeed there could be such a thing. Studying philosophy isn't an alternative to studying art, literature, history, psychology, anthropology, sociology, politics, and science. These different subjects concentrate on different aspects of human life and provide different sorts of insight. Some aspects of anyone's life will defy philosophical analysis, and perhaps analysis of any other kind too. It is important, then, not to expect too much of philosophy.

B5 James Rachels, Active and passive euthanasia

From Peter Singer (ed.) (1986) *Applied Ethics*, Oxford, Oxford University Press, Chapter III, pp.29–35; first published in *The New England Journal of Medicine*, 1975, vol.292, pp.78–80.

The distinction between active and passive euthanasia is thought to be crucial for medical ethics. The idea is that it is permissible, at least in some cases, to withhold treatment and allow a patient to die, but it is never permissible to take any direct action designed to kill the patient. This doctrine seems to be accepted by most doctors, and it is endorsed in a statement adopted by the House of Delegates of the American Medical Association on 4 December 1973:

> The intentional termination of the life of one human being by another – mercy killing – is contrary to that for which the medical profession stands and is contrary to the policy of the American Medical Association.

> The cessation of the employment of extraordinary means to prolong the life of the body when there is irrefutable evidence that biological death is imminent is the decision of the patient and/or his immediate family. The advice and judgement of the physician should be freely available to the patient and/or his immediate family.

However, a strong case can be made against this doctrine. In what follows I will set out some of the relevant arguments, and urge doctors to reconsider their views on this matter.

To begin with a familiar type of situation, a patient who is dying of incurable cancer of the throat is in terrible pain, which can no longer be satisfactorily alleviated. He is certain to die within a few days, even if present treatment is continued, but he does not want to go on living for those days since the pain is unbearable. So he asks the doctor for an end to it, and his family joins in the request.

Suppose the doctor agrees to withhold treatment, as the conventional doctrine says he may. The justification for his doing so is that the patient is in terrible agony, and since he is going to die anyway, it would be wrong to prolong his suffering needlessly. But now notice this. If one simply withholds treatment, it may take the patient longer to die, and so he may suffer more than he would if more direct action were taken and a lethal injection given. This fact provides strong reason for thinking that, once the initial decision not to prolong his agony has been made, active euthanasia is actually preferable to passive euthanasia, rather than the reverse. To say otherwise is to endorse the option that leads to more suffering rather than less, and is contrary to the humanitarian impulse that prompts the decision not to prolong his life in the first place.

Part of my point is that the process of being 'allowed to die' can be relatively slow and painful, whereas being given a lethal injection is relatively quick and painless. Let me give a different sort of example. In the United States about one in 600 babies is born with Down's syndrome. Most of these babies are otherwise healthy – that is, with only the usual pediatric care, they will proceed to an otherwise normal infancy. Some, however, are born with congenital defects such as intestinal obstructions that require operations if they are to live. Sometimes, the parents and the doctor will decide not to operate, and let the infant die. Anthony Shaw describes what happens then:

> When surgery is denied (the doctor) must try to keep the infant from suffering while natural forces sap the baby's life away. As a surgeon whose natural inclination is to use the scalpel to fight off death, standing by and watching a salvageable baby die is the most emotionally exhausting experience I know. It is easy at a conference, in a theoretical discussion to decide that such infants should be allowed to die. It is altogether different to stand by in the nursery and watch as dehydration and infection wither a tiny being over hours and days. This is a terrible ordeal for me and the hospital staff – much more so than for the parents who never set foot in the nursery.

I can understand why some people are opposed to all euthanasia, and insist that such infants must be allowed to live. I think I can also understand why other people favour destroying these babies quickly and painlessly. But why should anyone favour letting 'dehydration and infection wither a tiny being over hours and days'? The doctrine that says a baby may be allowed to dehydrate and wither, but may not be given an injection that would end its life without suffering, seems so patently cruel as to require no further refutation. The strong language is not intended to offend, but only to put the point in the clearest possible way.

My second argument is that the conventional doctrine leads to decisions concerning life and death made on irrelevant grounds.

Consider again the case of the infants with Down's syndrome who need operations for congenital defects unrelated to the syndrome to live. Sometimes, there is no operation, and the baby dies, but when there is no such defect, the baby lives on. Now, an operation such as that to remove an intestinal obstruction is not prohibitively difficult. The reason why such operations are not performed in these cases is, clearly, that the child has Down's syndrome and the parents and the doctor judge that because of that fact it is better for the child to die.

But notice that this situation is absurd, no matter what view one takes of the lives and potentials of such babies. If the life of such an infant is worth preserving what does it matter if it needs a simple operation? Or, if one thinks it better that such a baby should not live on, what difference does it make that it happens to have an unobstructed intestinal tract? In either case, the matter of life and death is being decided on irrelevant grounds. It is the Down's syndrome, and not the intestines, that is the issue. The matter should be decided, if at all, on that basis, and not be allowed to depend on the essentially irrelevant question of whether the intestinal tract is blocked.

What makes this situation possible, of course, is the idea that when there is an intestinal blockage, one can 'let the baby die', but when there is no such defect there is nothing that can be done, for one must not 'kill' it. The fact that this idea leads to such results as deciding life or death on irrelevant grounds is another good reason why the doctrine would be rejected.

One reason why so many people think that there is an important moral difference between active and passive euthanasia is that they think killing someone is morally worse than letting someone die. But is it? Is killing, in itself, worse than letting die? To investigate this issue, two cases may be considered that are exactly alike except that one involves killing whereas the other involves letting someone die. Then, it can be asked whether this difference makes any difference to the moral assessments. It is important that the cases be exactly alike, except for this one difference, since otherwise one cannot be confident that it is this difference and not some other that accounts for any variation in the assessments of the two cases. So, let us consider this pair of cases:

In the first, Smith stands to gain a large inheritance if anything should happen to his six-year-old cousin. One evening while the child is taking his bath, Smith sneaks into the bathroom and drowns the child, and then arranges things so that it will look like an accident.

In the second, Jones also stands to gain if anything should happen to his six-year-old cousin. Like Smith, Jones sneaks in planning to drown the child in his bath. However, just as he enters the bathroom Jones sees the child slip and hit his head, and fall face down in the water. Jones is delighted; he stands by, ready to push the child's head back under if it is necessary, but it is not necessary. With only a little thrashing about, the child drowns all by himself, 'accidentally', as Jones watches and does nothing.

Now Smith killed the child, whereas Jones 'merely' let the child die. That is the only difference between them. Did either man behave better, from a moral point of view? If the difference between killing and letting die were in itself a morally important matter, one should say that Jones's behaviour was less reprehensible than Smith's. But does one really want to say that? I think not. In the first place, both men acted from the same motive, personal gain, and both had exactly the same end in view when they acted. It may be inferred from Smith's conduct that he is a bad man, although that judgement may be withdrawn or modified if certain further facts are learned about him – for example, that he is mentally deranged. But would not the very same thing be inferred about Jones from his conduct? And would not the same further considerations also be relevant to any modification of this judgement? Moreover, suppose Jones pleaded, in his own defence, 'After all, I didn't do anything except just stand there and watch the child drown. I didn't kill him; I only let him die.' Again, if letting die were in itself less bad than killing, this defence should have at least some weight. But it does not. Such a 'defence' can only be regarded as a grotesque perversion of moral reasoning. Morally speaking, it is no defence at all.

Now, it may be pointed out, quite properly, that the cases of euthanasia with which doctors are concerned are not like this at all. They do not involve personal gain or the destruction of normal healthy children. Doctors are concerned only with cases in which the patient's life is of no further use to him, or in which the patient's life has become or will soon become a terrible burden. However, the point is the same in these cases: the bare difference between killing and letting die does not, in itself, make a moral difference. If a doctor lets a patient die, for humane reasons, he is in the same moral position as if he had given the patient a lethal injection for humane reasons. If his decision was wrong – if, for example, the patient's illness was in fact curable – the decision would be equally regrettable no matter which method was used to carry it out. And if the doctor's decision was the right one, the method used is not in itself important.

The AMA policy statement isolates the crucial issue very well; the crucial issue is 'the intentional termination of the life of one human being by another'. But after identifying this issue, and forbidding 'mercy killing', the statement goes on to deny that the cessation of treatment is the intentional termination of a life. This is where the mistake comes in, for what is the cessation of treatment, in these circumstances, if it is not 'the intentional termination of the life of one human being by another'? Of course it is exactly that, and if it were not, there would be no point to it.

Many people will find this judgement hard to accept. One reason, I think, is that it is very easy to conflate the question of whether killing is, in itself, worse than letting die, with the very different question of whether most actual cases of killing are more reprehensible than most actual cases of letting die. Most actual cases of killing are clearly terrible (think, for example, of all the murders reported in the newspapers), and one hears of such cases every day. On the other hand, one hardly ever hears of a case of letting die, except for the actions of doctors who are motivated by humanitarian reasons. So one learns to think of killing in much worse light than of letting die. But this does not mean that there is something about killing that makes it in itself worse than letting die, for it is not the bare difference between killing and letting die that makes the difference in these cases. Rather, the other factors – the murderer's motive of personal gain, for example, contrasted with the doctor's humanitarian motivation – account for different reactions to the different cases.

I have argued that killing is not in itself any worse than letting die; if my contention is right, it follows that active euthanasia is not any worse than passive euthanasia. What arguments can be given on the other side? The most common, I believe, is the following:

> The important difference between active and passive euthanasia is that, in passive euthanasia, the doctor does not do anything to bring about the patient's death. The doctor does nothing, and the patient dies of whatever ills already afflict him. In active euthanasia, however, the doctor does something to bring about the patient's death: he kills him. The doctor who gives the patient with cancer a lethal injection has himself caused his patient's death; whereas if he merely ceases treatment, the cancer is the cause of the death.

A number of points need to be made here. The first is that it is not exactly correct to say that in passive euthanasia the doctor does nothing, for he does do one thing that is very important: he lets the patient die. 'Letting someone die' is certainly different, in some respects, from other types of action – mainly in that it is a kind of action that one may perform by way of not performing certain other actions. For example, one may let a patient die by way of not giving medication, just as one may insult someone by way of not shaking his hand. But for any purpose of moral assessment, it is a type of action none the less. The decision to let a patient die is subject to moral appraisal in the same way that a decision to kill him would be subject to moral appraisal: it may be assessed as wise or unwise, compassionate or sadistic, right or wrong. If a doctor deliberately let a patient die who was suffering from a routinely curable illness, the doctor would certainly be to blame for what he had done, just as he would be to blame if he had needlessly killed the patient. Charges against him would then be appropriate. If so, it would be no defence at all for him to insist that he didn't 'do anything'. He would have done something very serious indeed, for he let his patient die.

Fixing the cause of death may be very important from a legal point of view, for it may determine whether criminal charges are brought against the doctor. But I do not think that this notion can be used to show a moral difference between active and passive euthanasia. The reason why it is considered bad to be the cause of someone's death is that death is regarded as a great evil – and so it is. However, if it has been decided that euthanasia – even passive euthanasia – is desirable in a given case, it has also been decided that in this instance death is no greater an evil than the patient's continued existence. And if this is true, the usual reason for not wanting to be the cause of someone's death simply does not apply.

Finally, doctors may think that all of this is only of academic interest – the sort of thing that philosophers may worry about but that has no practical bearing on their own work. After all, doctors must be concerned about the legal consequences of what they do, and active euthanasia is clearly forbidden by the law. But even so, doctors should also be concerned with the fact that the law is forcing upon them a moral doctrine that may be indefensible, and has a considerable effect on their practices. Of course, most doctors are not now in the position of being coerced in this matter, for they do not regard themselves as merely going along with what the law requires. Rather, in statements such as the AMA policy statement that I have quoted, they are endorsing this doctrine as a central point of medical ethics. In that statement, active euthanasia is condemned not merely as illegal but as 'contrary to that for which the medical profession stands', whereas passive euthanasia is approved. However, the preceding considerations suggest that there is really no moral difference between the two, considered in themselves (there may be important moral differences in some cases in their *consequences*, but, as I pointed out, these differences may make active euthanasia, and not passive euthanasia, the morally preferable option). So, whereas doctors may have to discriminate between active and passive euthanasia to satisfy the law, they should not do any more than that. In particular, they should not give the distinction any added authority and weight by writing it into official statements of medical ethics.

Section C CLASSICS: THE COLOSSEUM

Paula James, Introduction to Section C

The first group of texts in Section C (C1–C10) contains the ancient sources referred to throughout the discussion of the games (in Block 2 and on Cassette 3). Each of these texts includes a brief biography of the author which should help you to place their lives and works in historical context. The chronological survey on pages 89–91 will enable you to relate the authors to key dates and events of Roman history.

The secondary material (modern authors discussing issues about the games and Roman society) (C11–C16) does not all have to be thoroughly digested during your week's work on Block 2. Wiedemann's *Omnibus* article is a key text (C11) and you are also asked to read the short extract from Pearson (C12). The remaining selections are there as a resource for you and your tutor to refer to and select from during tutorial discussion. The extracts can be powerful, controversial and disturbing in the ethical questions they raise, for example the extinction of species, torture and death as theatrical entertainment, the dehumanization of 'deviants'. TV programme 7 invites leading scholars of the ancient world to exchange views on the society and attitudes of Rome.

The secondary material is taken from academic books and articles from Classical journals which were originally published with scholarly apparatus, that is with full references and footnotes. These elements have largely been omitted for ease of use in the context of A103. You should bear in mind, however, that the authors have researched their propositions thoroughly and they have drawn on a range of ancient texts and modern scholarship to substantiate their line of argument.

Important stages in Roman history

509 BCE Etruscan kings expelled from Rome and a republic with a ruling (aristocratic) senate and two annually elected consuls established. Rome starts expanding its territory across Italy.

Third century BCE Rome defeated Carthage and established colonies around the east and west Mediterranean, Spain, Africa, Greece and Asia. Rome was by this time a powerful empire but still had senatorial government rather than an emperor at the helm.

Second and first centuries BCE The Roman republican system was showing signs of strain. Powerful generals, with Roman legions to back them and with property and influence in the provinces, started to make their political presence felt in the capital. Famous names of the 60s and 50s BCE were Pompey and Julius Caesar. Caesar was *de facto* dictator of Rome from 49 to 44 BCE.

31 BCE Mark Antony defeated at Actium by Julius Caesar's heir, Octavian, later known as Augustus. Octavian became the first emperor of the Roman world, bringing the army and all the Roman political and legal institutions into his personal sphere of influence and control. From this point on, Roman rulers can conveniently be divided into imperial dynasties.

JULIO CLAUDIANS

27 BCE	Octavian becomes Augustus, first emperor
14 CE	Death of Augustus
14–37 CE	Tiberius emperor
37–41 CE	Gaius 'Caligula'
41–54 CE	Claudius
54–68 CE	Nero

FLAVIANS AND ANTONINES

68–69 CE	Galba
69 CE	Year of the Four Emperors: Galba, Otho, Vitellius, Vespasian
69–79 CE	Vespasian
79–81 CE	Titus
81–96 CE	Domitian
96–8 CE	Nerva
98–117 CE	Trajan
117–38 CE	Hadrian
138–61 CE	Antoninus Pius
161–80 CE	Marcus Aurelius (with Lucius Verus 161–9)
176–93 CE	Commodus (co-emperor 176–80)

SEVERAN DYNASTY

193 CE	Pertinax
193 CE	Didius Julianus
193–211 CE	Septimius Severus
211–17 CE	Caracalla
217–18 CE	Macrinus
218–22 CE	Elagabalus
222–35 CE	Alexander Severus

From 235 CE the Empire, its boundaries and rule at Rome were all far less stable. It proved administratively more flexible to have Emperors East and West throughout much of this period. Constantine was sole ruler

from 324 and in the famous Council of Nicaea in 325 he encouraged the unity of the church and promoted Christianity throughout the Empire. You will find some references to key events, figures and authors of the later Empire throughout Block 2.

Important dates for the Colosseum

71 CE	Building started by the Emperor Vespasian.
75	Vespasian dedicated first three stages.
80	The Emperor Titus (Vespasian's son and successor) dedicated building; but it was completed by the Emperor Domitian (Titus' brother and successor).
217	Badly damaged by fire in a storm.
222–3	Restored to use by the Emperor Alexander Severus, but repairs not completed until 241–4
250 or 252	Further damage by lightning, repaired again.
410	Sack of Rome by Alaric and the Goths.
434–5	Last known gladiatorial combats took place, but wild-beast hunts continued to 523.
442 and 484 (or 508)	Damage by earthquakes, followed by restoration.

C1   Martial, On the spectacles

From G.P. Gould (ed.) (1993) *Martial Epigrams*, translated by D.R. Shackleton Bailey, Loeb Classical Library, Cambridge, Mass., Harvard University Press, vol.I.

Martial (40–103/104 CE): Marcus Valerius Martialis was born in north-east Spain and may have had family connections with Seneca. He made a name for himself as a writer of epigrams (a Greek verse form consisting of short poems directed to love, wine, useful also for compliments and insults, testaments to friendship and observations on life in general). Martial's Book of Shows *brought him very much into the public eye. Half of the original series is missing but the surviving text gives us the flavour of the work and is invaluable as a source for the Colosseum.*

1

Let barbarous Memphis speak no more of the wonder of her pyramids, nor Assyrian[1] toil boast of Babylon; nor let the soft Ionians be extolled for Trivia's temple;[2] let the altar of many horns[3] say naught of Delos; nor let the Carians exalt to the skies with extravagant praises the Mausoleum poised in empty air. All labor yields to Caesar's Amphitheater.[4] Fame shall tell of one work in lieu of all.

2

Where the starry colossus[5] sees the constellations at close range and lofty scaffolding[6] rises in the middle of the road, once gleamed the odious halls of a cruel monarch, and in all Rome there stood a single house.[7] Where rises before our eyes the august pile of the Amphitheater, was once Nero's lake. Where we admire the warm baths,[8] a speedy gift, a haughty tract of land had robbed the poor of their dwellings. Where the Claudian colonnade unfolds its wide-spread shade, was the outermost part of the palace's[9] end. Rome has been restored to herself, and under your rule, Caesar, the pleasances that belonged to a master now belong to the people.

3

Believe that Pasiphae was mated to the Dictaean bull; we have seen it, the old legend has won credence. And let not hoary antiquity plume itself, Caesar: whatever Fame sings of, the arena affords you.

4

It is not enough that warrior Mars serves you in unconquered arms, Caesar. Venus herself serves you too.[10]

5

Illustrious Fame used to sing of the lion laid low in Nemea's spacious vale, Hercules' work. Let ancient testimony be silent, for after your shows, Caesar, we have now seen such things done by women's valor.

6

As Prometheus, bound on Scythian crag, fed the tireless bird with his too abundant breast, so did Laureolus,[11] hanging on no sham cross, give his naked flesh to a Caledonian boar. His lacerated limbs lived on, dripping gore, and in all his body, body there was none. Finally he met with the punishment he deserved; the guilty wretch had plunged a sword into his father's throat or his master's, or in his madness had robbed a temple of its secret gold, or laid a cruel torch to Rome. The criminal had outdone the misdeeds of ancient history; in him, what had been a play became an execution.

7

A treacherous lion had harmed his master with his ingrate mouth, daring to violate the hands he knew so well; but he paid a fitting penalty for such a crime, and suffered weapons who had not suffered stripes. What should be the manners of men under such a prince, who commands wild beasts to be of milder nature?

8

A wild sow, now pregnant, sent forth her progeny, pledge of her ripe womb, made parent by a wound. Nor did the offspring lie on the ground, but ran as the mother fell. How ingenious are sudden chances!

9

Devoted and suppliant the elephant adores you, Caesar, he who but lately was so formidable to the bull. He does it unbidden, no master teaches him. Believe me, he too feels our god.

10

A tigress, wont to lick the hand of the fearless trainer, rare glory from Hyrcanian mountains, fiercely tore a wild lion with rabid tooth; a novelty, unknown in any times. She dared do no such thing while she lived in the high forests, but since she has been among us she has gained ferocity.

11

If you are here from distant land, a late spectator for whom this was the first day of the sacred[12] show, let not the naval warfare deceive you with its ships, and the water like to a sea:[13] here but lately was land. You don't believe it? Watch while the waters weary Mars.[14] But a short while hence you will be saying: 'Here but lately was sea.'

[1] That is, Babylonian, by a license common in Latin poetry.

[2] The temple of Diana at Ephesus.

[3] Constructed by Apollo of the horns of the beasts slain by his sister Diana. Like the other items, reckoned as one of the wonders of the world.

[4] The Flavian Amphitheater, later called the Colosseum, begun by Vespasian and finished by Titus.

[5] A colossal statue of Nero, transferred from its place in his Golden House to the Via Sacra by Vespasian, who replaced the head to make it into a statue of the Sun, complete with rays.

[6] The purpose of this is in doubt.

[7] The Golden House of Nero, built in 64 CE after the great fire of Rome.

[8] Of Titus, one of Rome's three great public baths, along with those of Agrippa and Nero. Martial regularly refers to these as *thermae* ('warm baths') as distinct from privately built and owned establishments (*balnea*).

[9] The Golden House.

[10] Women sometimes fought in the arena; see the next epigram.

[11] A robber who had been crucified and torn to pieces by wild beasts. A mime on the subject was performed under Caligula. The death was now enacted 'for real' by a criminal in the amphitheater.

[12] Because the Emperor gave it and was present in person.

[13] The arena had been flooded to stage a mock sea fight.

[14] While the sea fight lasts.

C2 Apuleius, The ass in the arena

From A. Hanson (ed.) (1989) *Apuleius Metamorphoses*, Loeb Classical Library, Cambridge, Mass., Harvard University Press, 2 vols, *Metamorphoses*, X, vol.2.

Apuleius (born c.125 CE, date of death unknown): Apuleius was a native of Numidia, the Roman province of North Africa. He studied at Carthage and Athens, receiving commemorative statues for his fine speeches at Carthage. He was a renowned orator, a philosopher and a novelist who wrote in richly stylized Latin. His novel, The Golden Ass *or* Metamorphoses, *has been recently reissued by Penguin in the popular translation by Robert Graves, the author of* I, Claudius.

[The young man Lucius, transformed into an ass, narrates his adventures.]

And now a solider came hurrying across the theatre floor in answer to the audience's demands, to fetch the woman from the public prison, the one who I told you had been condemned to the beasts for her manifold crimes and engaged to make an illustrious match with me. And now a bed, evidently meant to serve as our honeymoon couch, was being elaborately made up, shining with Indian tortoise-shell, piled high with a feathered mattress, and spread with a flowery silk coverlet.

But as for me, besides my shame at indulging in sexual intercourse in public, besides the contagion of this damnable polluted woman, I was greatly tormented by the fear of death; for I thought to myself that, when we were in fact fastened together in Venus' embrace, any wild animal that might be let in to slaughter the woman could not possibly turn out to be so intelligently clever or so skilfully educated or so temperately moderate as to mangle the woman lying attached to my loins while sparing me on the grounds that I was unconvicted and innocent. So now I was afraid not for my honour, but for my very life. While my trainer gave his full attention to the proper fitting of our couch, and all the slaves were busy, some occupied with preparations for the hunting-spectacle, the others spellbound by the sensual pleasure of the show, I was allowed free rein for my own devices.

C3   Apuleius, 'The robbers' tale'

From A. Hanson (ed.) (1989) *Apuleius Metamorphoses*, Loeb Classical Library, Cambridge, Mass., Harvard University Press, 2 vols, *Metamorphoses*, X, vol.1.

There we picked up the current talk about a certain Demochares[1] who was about to produce a gladiatorial show. A man of high birth, great wealth and liberality, he was preparing a public entertainment of a brilliance to match his fortune. Who has enough talent, enough eloquence, to find the right words to describe each item of the elaborate show? There were gladiators of renowned strength, animal-hunters of proven agility, and criminals, too, without hope of reprieve, who were to provide a banquet of themselves to fatten the beasts. There was also an articulated contrivance made of wood, towers formed of scaffolding rather like houses on wheels, coloured with gay paintings, ornamental cages for the beasts to be hunted. And oh the quantity and fine appearance of the wild beasts! For he had taken great pains and had even imported from abroad these noble sepulchres for the condemned men. Beside the other furnishings for this showy spectacle, he employed the total resources of his inheritance to collect a large band of enormous bears. In addition to those hunted and captured by his own staff and those acquired by expensive purchases, others had been presented to him by friends vying with one another in their various gifts. He lavishly tended and fed all those bears with the utmost care.

But such grand and splendid preparations for the public's pleasure did not escape the baleful eyes of Envy. The bears, exhausted by their lengthy captivity, emaciated from the burning summer heat, and listless from their sedentary inactivity, were attacked by a sudden epidemic and had their numbers reduced almost to nothing. You could see the animal wreckage of their moribund carcasses lying scattered in most of the streets.

[1] His name means 'People-pleaser'.

C4   Pliny the Younger, Letter to Valerius Maximus

From *The Letters of the Younger Pliny*, translated by Betty Radice, Harmondsworth, Penguin, 1963, Book 6, Letter 34.

Pliny the Younger (61–112 CE): Pliny was a member of the Italian municipal aristocracy at Como. He survived as a senator at Rome through the harsh reign of Domitian. Pliny is particularly famous for his correspondence with the Emperor Trajan, which includes letters about the problems posed by the Christians in the province of Bithynia (where he was governor from 110). He wrote many letters to friends and revised these for publication, organizing them by themes, topics, historical events and court activities.

You did well to put on a show of gladiators for our people of Verona, who have long shown their affection and admiration for you and have voted you many honours. Verona was also the home town of the excellent wife you loved so dearly, whose memory you owe some public building or show, and this kind of spectacle is particularly suitable for a funeral tribute. Moreover, the request came from so many people that a refusal would have been judged churlish rather than strong-minded on your part. You have also done admirably in giving the show so readily and on such a lavish scale, for this indicates a true spirit of generosity.

I am sorry the African panthers you had bought in such quantities did not turn up on the appointed day, but you deserve the credit although the weather prevented their arriving in time; it was not your fault that you could not show them.

C5 Suetonius, The Emperor Titus

From Suetonius, *Lives of the Twelve Caesars*, W. Heinemann (ed.), translated by J.C. Rolfe, Loeb Classical Library, Cambridge, Mass., Harvard University Press, 2 vols, vol.2, paragraphs 7 and 8.

Suetonius (c.70–c.160 CE): Suetonius rose to be an imperial secretary under Trajan and devoted his later years to historical and antiquarian study. The Lives of the Caesars *is the only work of his that has survived complete. The report on Titus sounds factual but Suetonius was only ten years old at the time of the inaugural games. He might even be drawing on Martial's poetry to fill out the picture and to supplement his own memories and the eye-witness accounts he could have collected.*

Ancient biographers, and Suetonius was no exception, were men of the educated upper class and regarded the lives of the emperors as 'the main thread of history'. The exploits of great men at home and abroad were used as illustrations of human weakness and human triumph and success. Suetonius does not short change us on salacious stories about the emperors. Robert Graves translated his Twelve Caesars *for the Penguin edition and used him as a major source for his historical novels,* I, Claudius *and* Claudius the God. *It is perhaps not surprising that this account of imperial fortunes made for excellent upmarket soap opera on BBC television in the 1970s.*

[Y]et he would second to none of his predecessors in munificence. At the dedication of the amphitheatre and of the baths which were hastily built near it he gave a most magnificent and costly gladiatorial show.

The whole body of the people in particular he treated with such indulgence on all occasions that once at a gladiatorial show he declared that he would give it, 'not after his own inclinations but those of the spectators'; and what is more he kept his word.

C6   Cicero, Pompey's shows

From Cicero, *Letters to his Friends*, Betty Radice (ed.), Harmondsworth, Penguin, 1978, 2 vols, vol.1, Letter 7.1.

Cicero (104–43 BCE): Cicero was an orator and politician who lived in the turbulent times of the late Republic. He welcomed Julius Caesar's assassination in 44 but later fell victim to the Second Triumvirate, a carving up of power between Mark Antony, Lepidus and the young Octavian. Cicero published many of his polemical and legal speeches, rhetorical and philosophical works and a number of poems. His sixteen books of letters give an intimate picture of the private as well as the public man.

There remain the animal-hunts, twice daily for five days – very lavish, no one denies. But what pleasure can it be to a man of refinement when either a powerless man is torn by a very powerful beast, or else a magnificent beast is spitted on a hunting-spear? In any case, if such things are worth seeing, you have seen them often; and we who were there saw nothing new. The last day was devoted to the elephants. The sight caused great astonishment among the common herd, but there was no pleasure in it; indeed there was a reaction almost to pity, and a kind of feeling that this animal had something in common with the human race.

C7   Statius, The tame lion

From Statius, *Silvae*, W. Heineman (ed.), translated by J.H. Mozley, Loeb Classical Library, Cambridge, Mass., Harvard University Press, 1928, V.

*Statius (40/45–c.96 CE): Statius' family was from Naples and he became a well established writer in the reign of Domitian. He wrote epics, panegyrics and a collection of shorter poems (*Silvae*) which demonstrate his skill with metre and his wide learning. He was adept at producing poems for the occasion, particularly events in the life of the Emperor's court.*

V. The tame lion

What now has it availed thee to quell thy rage and be tamed, to unlearn crime and human slaughter from thy heart, and endure dominion and obey a lesser lord? To have been wont to leave thy cage and return again to imprisonment, and of thy own will yield up the captured prey, to open thy jaws and let go the inserted hand? Thou art fallen, O skilled slayer of tall beasts, not caught within the enclosing circle of a Massylian hunting-band, nor flinging thyself with dreaded spring against the spears, nor deceived by the hidden yawning of a pit, but overcome by a beast that fled thee. The unlucky cage stands open, while behind their barriers all around the quiet lions grew wrathful that so great a wrong should have been suffered. Then all their crests fell, and shame came on them to see the corpse brought back, and they drew down all their brows upon their eyes. Yet when the first stroke o'erthrew thee the unwonted shame o'erwhelmed thee not: thy valour remained, and even in the hour of death thy brave spirit rallied as thou didst fall, nor did all thy fierceness straightway own defeat. Just as the dying warrior who knows his wound is mortal yet goes against the foe, and lifts his hand to strike, and threatens even while the weapon falls from his grasp; so he with laboured step and reft of his wonted pride steadies his eyes as with open mouth he pants for breath and for the foe.

Great solace, nevertheless, shall be thine, poor victim, for thy sudden fate, that people and Senate mourned in sorrow to see thee die, as though thou wert some favourite gladiator fallen on the deadly sand; that amid so many beasts of Scythia and Libya, from the banks of Rhine and the tribes of Egypt, beasts so cheaply slain, the loss of one lion alone drew a tear from mighty Caesar's eye.

C8 Cicero, Philosophical discussion

From Cicero, *Tusculan Disputations*, translated by G.E. King, Loeb Classical Library, Cambridge, Mass., Harvard University Press, 1927, 2.41.

I know that in the eyes of some people the gladiatorial combats are a cruel and inhuman spectacle; and perhaps they are not wrong considering the way in which the combats are given today. But in the days when it was criminals who killed one another, no lesson in how to endure in the face of pain and death could be more efficacious, at least among those addressed not to the ears but to the eyes. [...] These gladiators, these rogues, these barbarians to what lengths do they carry their strength of mind.

C9 Seneca, Letter 7

From Seneca, *17 Letters*, translated by C.D.N Costa, Warminster, Aris-Phillips, 1988, Letter 7.

Seneca (date of birth uncertain, died 65 CE): Philosopher and politician, Seneca virtually ruled Rome for five years on behalf of the young Emperor Nero. He was a prolific writer – tragedies, many ethical dialogues, consolations and moral letters. He was implicated in the conspiracy of Piso and forced to commit suicide by the Emperor.

You ask me what you should regard as particularly to be avoided. A crowd. You can't yet safely entrust yourself to it. At any rate I will confess my own weakness: I never come home with the same moral character I set out with. Some of the peace of mind I have achieved is disturbed, one or other of those things which I have banished returns. You know how invalids are so reduced by prolonged weakness that they cannot venture outside without ill effects: it is the same with those of us who are recovering from a long spiritual illness. Associating with crowds is dangerous: someone is bound to seduce us with some vice, or stamp or smear it on us even without our being conscious of it. Obviously the larger the crowd the greater the danger of this. Indeed there is nothing so damaging to good character as to take a seat at a show, for then faults sneak up on us more easily through our enjoyment. Do you think I mean that I go home more greedy, more ambitious, more self-indulgent? Yes – and more cruel and inhuman because I have been among humans.

I happened to drop in on a midday show, looking for entertainment, wit, and some relaxation in which human eyes could take a rest from human blood. It was quite the opposite. All the fights beforehand were acts of mercy in comparison: now the frivolities are banished and we are offered sheer butchery. The combatants wear no protection: their whole bodies are exposed to strokes and they never aim a blow in vain. Most of the spectators prefer this to the regular matches and the special demand ones. Naturally: there's neither helmet nor shield to ward off the weapon. What's the point of protection or skill? All that just delays death. In the morning men are thrown to lions and bears and at midday to their own spectators. The crowd insists that those who have killed their man are thrown against those who will kill them in turn, and reserves each victor for another slaughter. The only outcome for the combatants is death, while fire and steel keep things moving. All this happens between the main shows. 'But', you say, 'the man was a brigand, a murderer.' So what? Because he killed he deserved this fate; but what have *you* done, poor wretch, to deserve this spectacle? 'Kill him, beat him, burn him! Why is he so fearful of running against the sword? Why does he kill so timidly? Why is he so loth to die? Let him be driven by blows to receive his wounds; let them face and batter each other with unprotected breasts.' And when there's an interval: 'Let some throats be cut meanwhile, to keep things going'. Come now, don't you even know this, that evil examples recoil on those who offer them? Give the immortal gods thanks that you are giving a lesson in cruelty to a man who cannot learn it.

C10 St Augustine, The story of Alypius

From St Augustine, *Confessions*, R. Baldick (ed.), translated by R.S. Pine Coffin, Harmondsworth, Penguin, 1961, VI.8.

St Augustine (354–430 CE): Renowned as a great philosopher of the Western church, Augustine had been converted to Christianity in 386 and adopted a monastic life from 387. His consecration as bishop of Hippo (North Africa) brought him very much into public and political life and current church disputes. He reviewed his enormous literary output – treatises, sermons, letters – in 426 towards the end of his life.

He became obsessed with an extraordinary craving for gladiatorial shows. At first he detested these displays and refused to attend them. But one day during the season for this cruel and bloodthirsty sport he happened to meet some friends and fellow-students returning from their dinner. In a friendly way they brushed aside his resistance and his stubborn protests and carried him off to the arena.

'You may drag me there bodily,' he protested, 'but do you imagine that you can make me watch the show and give my mind to it? I shall be there, but it will be just as if I were not present, and I shall prove myself stronger than you or the games.'

He did not manage to deter them by what he said, and perhaps the very reason why they took him with them was to discover whether he would be as good as his word. When they arrived at the arena, the place was seething with the lust for cruelty. They found seats as best they could and Alypius shut his eyes tightly, determined to have nothing to do with these atrocities. If only he had closed his ears as well! For an incident in the fight drew a great roar from the crowd, and this thrilled him so deeply that he could not contain his curiosity. Whatever had caused the uproar, he was confident that, if he saw it, he would find it repulsive and remain master of himself. So he opened his eyes, and his soul was stabbed with a wound more deadly than any which the gladiator, whom he was so anxious to see, had received in his body. He fell, and fell more pitifully than the man whose fall had drawn that roar of excitement from the crowd. The din had pierced his ears and forced him to open his eyes, laying his soul open to receive the wound which struck it down. This was presumption, not courage. The weakness of his soul was in relying upon itself instead of trusting in you.

When he saw the blood, it was as though he had drunk a deep draught of savage passion. Instead of turning away, he fixed his eyes upon the scene and drank in all its frenzy, unaware of what he was doing. He revelled in the wickedness of the fighting and was drunk with the fascination of bloodshed. He was no longer the man who had come to the arena, but simply one of the crowd which he had joined, a fit companion for the friends who had brought him.

Need I say more? He watched and cheered and grew hot with excitement, and when he left the arena, he carried away with him a diseased mind which would leave him no peace until he came back again, no longer simply together with the friends who had first dragged him there, but at their head, leading new sheep to the slaughter. Yet you stretched out your almighty, ever merciful hand, O God, and rescued him from this madness. You taught him to trust in you, not in himself. But this was much later.

C11 Thomas Wiedemann, Emperors, gladiators and Christians

From *Omnibus*, September 1991, Issue 22, pp.26–8.

Wiedemann's article was originally published in Omnibus *with three supporting illustrations. Three illustrations of the same subjects are also printed here, but you should note that the view of the amphitheatre at El Djem is not the same as in the original article and that a larger area of the Nennig mosaic is reproduced here.*

When we study the ancient Greeks and Romans, we cannot help making judgements about them. There are things that we find attractive about them, and others that are repulsive. That for many centuries the Romans (and in the course of time, many Greeks too) enjoyed watching men kill each other, and wild beasts, in the arena, is something that we find repulsive. But simply to give way to our emotions is not enough: if we are to understand the ancient world, we must also try to understand what we condemn, and why the Romans did not see what went on in the amphitheatre as something wicked.

The context of the Roman 'games' gives rise to a number of emotional reactions. There are humanitarian or environmental issues, to do with the killing of wild beasts (and of course the Spanish bullfights which continue the tradition of Roman animal-hunts, *venationes*, that often took place in the same arenas). There is the political issue of capital punishment. Our attitude to Christianity, and the Christian martyrs, is involved: the cross on which the Romans executed their slaves became the cross which the Popes had planted in the arena of Rome's Colosseum as a sign of Christianity's ultimate victory. In short, the subject is emotive because it impinges on some of the basic moral concerns of many of us today.

FIGURE 1   *Roman amphitheatre at El Djem, Tunisia. Photograph: A.F. Kersting.*

Romans and Greeks

It involved some of the Romans' basic values, too. We only have to look at the Colosseum to see how much effort a 'good' emperor like Vespasian was prepared to put into giving the Romans the best gladiatorial facilities. In his list of the Greatest Things He Did, the *Res gestae*, Augustus himself boasts that: 'On three occasions I gave a gladiatorial show on my own behalf and fifteen times on behalf of my sons or grandsons. About ten thousand men fought in these shows ...'. No self-respecting city anywhere in the western half of the empire could be without its amphitheatre, from the earth-and-wood structures we can visit at Cirencester and Caerleon to the stupendous ruin of El Djem on the edge of the Sahara. In 1988, archaeologists from the Museum of London found the remains of a massive amphitheatre beneath the Guildhall and adjacent buildings in the City of London.

If few such buildings were put in the Greek half of the empire, that was only because the Greeks already had plenty of theatres in which to put on their gladiatorian and wild-beast 'shows'. We can no longer accept the prejudice that Greeks were too civilized to approve of such spectacles – though philosophers, Romans as well as Greeks, pointed out that gladiatorial and wild-beast games, like strip-tease shows, tended to engage the emotions of the onlookers to an extent that made them temporarily incapable of rational thought. One of the finest accounts of how attending such a show perverted a man's reason occurs in St Augustine's *Confessions*: 'When he saw the blood, it was as though he had drunk a deep draught of savage passion. Instead of turning away, he fixed his eyes upon the scene and drank in all its frenzy, unaware of what he was doing. He revelled in the wickedness of the fighting and was drunk with the fascination of bloodshed'.

FIGURE 2   *Scenes from the amphitheatre on a third-century CE mosaic from the Roman villa at Nennig, Germany. Photograph: Bildarchiv Foto Marburg.*

The struggle with nature

People in the twentieth century have become aware of the objections to the indiscriminate killing of animals. For the Romans, the struggle against nature was very real. To kill wild beasts meant to protect mankind. A poem in the *Greek Anthology* actually heaps praises on an emperor for (it claims) having entirely eradicated the lion-population of North Africa. To have large numbers of wild beasts destroyed was something of which a good ruler should be proud. Augustus in his *Res gestae* again: 'I provided wild beast hunts with African animals twenty-six times in my own name or that of my sons or grandsons in the Circus or the Forum or in amphitheatres. In these shows, about three thousand five hundred animals were killed'.

Some emperors are reported to have appeared in the arena in person to kill wild beasts: Commodus in particular was rumoured to have been keen on decapitating ostriches by shooting sickle-headed arrows at them. Whatever the truth behind such tales, several emperors liked to see themselves as performing the services for humanity that Hercules had once performed: ridding the world of wild beasts, and establishing civilization (see the bust of Commodus as Hercules in the Conservatori Museum at Rome [Plate 29]).

Another aspect of Hercules' civilizing mission had been to rid the world of evil criminals. Only a few idealists will go so far as to deny that society ought, in some way, to punish criminals and eradicate crime. The arena was one place where Roman society dealt with them. It was a symbol of the ordered world, the 'cosmos'; and it was the emperor who was the guarantor of that order.

In the provinces, the execution of criminals, killing of wild beasts, and gladiatorial combat, all took place in association with cult-centres and ceremonies honouring the emperor. At Rome, these spectacles came to symbolize good government. The Colosseum was not just a monument to the successful suppression of the Jewish revolt, but also to the restoration of traditional Roman 'freedom' by Vespasian following the civil wars of AD 68–69 and the overthrow of Nero (it was built on the site of Nero's highly unpopular Golden House, on land that he had taken away from its owners after the great fire of AD 64).

Life and death

The arena was not only on the margin between culture and the wild, but also between life and death. Whatever the origins of these games (and ancient theories suggesting that they originated as funeral sacrifices imported from Etruria or Campania, or as a form of military exercise which came to be a substitute for warfare, are not necessarily reliable), in the imperial period we find them in association with the public execution of criminals of low status, principally criminal slaves.

Attitudes to executions were as ambivalent in antiquity as they are now; crime must be punished, but taking life is not something that people are prepared to do lightly. Societies have evolved different ways of avoiding the unease involved in capital punishment. The execution may be carried out by the community as a whole, or by several people at the same time (stoning, or the firing squad); the criminal himself may be forced to perform the act from which his death results (as Socrates was forced to drink hemlock). The criminal may be in some sense ejected from the community and left to the tender mercies of nature, so that the community does not directly take away the criminal's life, but stops protecting him from the power of nature. Hence the traditional Germanic method of execution; leaving the criminal hanging from an oak tree, sacred to Wodan, and letting nature take its course.

The punishment of criminals at Rome by throwing them to the wild beasts, tying them to a cross, or forcing two condemned criminals to fight each other as gladiators, was in principle no different. Heinous crimes like murder or arson excluded their perpetrators from any claim to the protection of human society. Those whom a court of law had found guilty of the violence of beasts were surrendered to the appropriate natural forces. Once condemned, they were physically still alive: but socially already dead. 'We who are about to die salute you.'

What made gladiators particularly fascinating – to Romans as much as to us was that criminals condemned *ad ludos*, to fight in the arena, were 'dead men' who might just come alive again. If they fought bravely enough, the community might be sufficiently impressed to be prepared to grant them their life back, by demanding that the giver of the games release them, and sometimes even give them their

FIGURE 3   *Relief fragment from the Tiber showing gladiators with helmets, shields and short swords, National Museum, Rome. Photograph: Ancient Art and Architecture Library, London.*

freedom. A brave fighter might rise from the dead, and rejoin the society of the living. That was not in the gift of the president of the games, magistrate or even emperor, but in the gift of society as a whole; of the Roman people, present in the amphitheatre. Gladiatorial games were ultimate democracy; the crowd decided who might live again.

Gentlemen and players

Not all gladiators were condemned criminals; some were men of free birth. Ancient sources stress the utter degradation of the professional gladiator; he must take an oath (and Roman oaths were terrifying) to obey his trainer or else accept punishments that might otherwise only be inflicted on a slave. We can only speculate about the reasons that would make a freeborn citizen sink so low; perhaps the loss of all his property in an unsuccessful lawsuit. Such gladiators may be compared with eighteenth-century highwaymen, often gentlemen who turned to crime because their only skill was fighting, or with the men who (even today) as a result of failure or scandal choose to exchange the society of their birth for a new identity in the French Foreign Legion.

Another group of those executed in the arena were defeated military opponents, enemies of the Romans who had refused to accept the benefits of subjection to Roman order. It is notorious that the Romans convinced themselves that no-one might legitimately oppose their rule: to fight Rome was to rebel. Such rebels had forfeited any right to a place within Roman society; they had excluded themselves from the community of civilized peoples, and deserved death.

Out of their clemency, the Romans might choose to give them a new life; they might 'save' them (Lat. *servare*) and make them slaves (*servi*); whatever the real etymology of the Latin word for slaves, Roman writers explicitly state that a slave is so-called because he has been 'saved' from the death he deserved. But if the enemy had behaved with atrocious barbarity, or perhaps was just too dangerous, the Romans felt they had every right not to exercise such clemency. Rebels deserved execution: that execution might be carried out by crucifixion, like that of Spartacus' defeated followers, or in the arena, like the killing of tens of thousands of Jewish prisoners of war in the games organized by Titus and Vespasian in the aftermath of the conquest of Jerusalem.

Condemnation to crucifixion, to death by being thrown to wild beasts, or to fighting as a gladiator: that is what you deserved if you had chosen to reject membership of the community of civilized Romans. The wicked and the rebellious had acted in a way that put them outside society. But there was another group whose loyalty to the community, to civilization as the Romans knew it, was suspect: Christians. Some Christians (but, we may note, only some, and these often disowned as extremists by their bishops) denied the validity of the secular state altogether. Such behaviour suggested that Christianity threatened the entire basis of Mediterranean civilization; if someone was loyal only to some otherworldly community, how could he be a useful citizen of the city where he had been born, and (perhaps a crucial point) for which he had the obligation to pay taxes and serve in the army? On infrequent but well-publicized occasions, the cry went up: *Christianos ad bestias* – 'throw the Christians to the lions'.

The symbolism of public execution in the arena – the appropriate penalty for rejecting the values of this secular world – became deeply ingrained in the consciousness of Christians. Many an aristocratic pagan girl with too much time on her hands dreamt of 'wrestling' with a gladiator; a graffito from Pompeii calls the gladiator Celadus *suspirium puellarum*, 'the girls' heart-throb'. The Christian martyr St Felicity dreamt before her execution in the amphitheatre at Carthage that she wrestled with a gladiator (a great big Ethiopian), and beat him, and that he was the devil, and that she received the victor's palm not from the Proconsul, but from Christ himself.

The victorious gladiator's palm-branch became the special mark of the martyr. But the supreme – extreme – sign of Christian victory was the Cross. Crucifixion was the ultimate degradation, a sign that the criminal had forfeited his right to be treated as a human being. For the Romans, it was the means of eliminating the rebel from human society. For Christians, it became a sign that through his degradation, their Saviour had overcome for all time the limitations both of human society, and of human nature.

C12 John Pearson, On the Colosseum

From J. Pearson (1973) *Arena: the story of the Colosseum*, New York, McGraw-Hill, pp.7–8.

In the year AD 80 the Colosseum opened with what must stand as quite the longest, most disgusting, organized mass binge in history. According to Suetonius, various sorts of large-scale slaughter, both of animals and of men, were appreciatively watched by the Emperor Titus and a packed audience for the next hundred days. All this was considered highly laudable, an extra-special celebration of the state, duly enhanced by the presence of Roman senators, court officials, priests, vestal virgins and sacred effigies of the gods. The Emperor Titus was quite happily footing the enormous bill, just as he and his father, the imperial Vespasian, had already footed the bill for building this vast arena. Such payments were the privilege of power; the new arena was officially the gift of the Emperor to the Roman people and would ensure his fame for ever.

Not that this worked. Officially the arena was called the Flavian Amphitheatre, after the dynastic name of the Emperor, but several centuries ahead it would pick up its simpler and more lasting title. Ironically this name, which would erase all mention of the Flavians from popular memory, had originated with their hated predecessor, Nero. His colossal statue stood near the site of the arena. Rather than demolish it, Vespasian had ingeniously changed its head and its identity to that of Apollo, the sun god. And it was this colossus, with Apollo's head, but built by Nero, that gave the arena its enduring name, the Colosseum.

The opening was a delirious affair, a mammoth celebration on the grandest scale. For something like six years Rome's citizens had watched an army of skilled workmen draining the lake of Nero's Golden House which occupied the site, preparing the immense foundations, then raising the walls. All this had started in the reign of Vespasian. That stingy but impressive Emperor was rebuilding Rome after the ravages of Nero's fire. He was determined that his city should recover its ancient splendour as the world's capital; the Colosseum, more than any other building, symbolized the massiveness, the power and sense of order of the new régime. One of the last acts of Vespasian's life was to dedicate it, proudly, in the year AD 79.

Titus succeeded him and piously continued work on the arena. From the scant evidence of the historians, Titus appears to have been one of the kindliest men to rule Rome. He is the emperor Suetonius describes complaining over supper of not having had a chance to do anyone a favour since the previous day. 'My friends,' the Emperor exclaimed, 'I have wasted a day.' And yet this kindly man shared his father's passion for the arena. Work on the Colosseum had been hurried on, and he clearly could not wait for the shows to start. As it was, the Colosseum was not completely finished for these celebrations; its fourth and final storey was to be added in the reign of the next Emperor, the unspeakable Domitian, last of the Flavians.

Despite this, Titus had lavished money on it. It was a show-piece, and must already have possessed something today's bare ruins make it hard to picture – a sense of ostentatious luxury. This was a vulgar age. Imperial Rome rejoiced in over-decoration and extravagance. The outside walls of the amphitheatre were plastered over the stonework, disguising the construction, niches were adorned with statues of the gods, the ceilings of the seventy-two public stairways were painted gold and purple, all inside walls were faced with marble.

C13 (a) and (b) Thomas Wiedemann, Emperors and gladiators

From T. Wiedemann (1992) *Emperors and Gladiators*, London, Routledge, pp.70–2, 150–2, 153.

Extract (a)

[T]his pain was not inflicted randomly or because it was enjoyed for its own sake, and therefore it is not appropriate to describe it as sadistic. Maximum cruelty was not exercised on every possible occasion; rather, the pain inflicted had to be commensurate with the suffering the criminal had caused, or might have caused, to others. A clear example is the burning alive of an adult convicted of setting fire to a temple or to a store of grain, already prescribed in the Law of the Twelve Tables. The jurist Ulpian says that *crematio* applies to those guilty of sacrilege, as well as rebels and deserters. The punishment might be inflicted on the part of the body through which the crime had been committed: as governor of Tarraconensis, Galba punished a fraudulent money-lender by amputating his hands and nailing him to his banker's table. Caligula paraded a criminal whose hands had been amputated through the city with a placard stating what his crime had been. The physical pain inflicted on the criminal was also intended to degrade him. An evil-doer may be perceived as someone who arrogates to himself certain rights which he does not have (rights to appropriate property belonging to another, for example, or the right to inflict harm on another person). In a society based on status differentiation, such an arrogation of rights is perceived as claiming a status to which the accused has no claim. His action thus overturns the proper hierarchy of statuses public recognition of which is essential if society is to function smoothly. The public humiliation of the criminal re-establishes social order by cancelling the criminal's exercise of rights which he did not have. The gospel narrative of the crucifixion provides a characteristic example: having been found guilty of claiming the status of king of the Jews, Jesus was humiliated by being dressed up as king in a cloak and crowned with a diadem of thorns.

The punishment of criminals does not simply concern the convict, his victims, and the state, but all those who share a particular society's's perceptions of what constitutes unacceptable behaviour subject to publicly proclaimed legal penalties. For the public to be reassured that the proper social order is indeed being restored by means of the inflicting of appropriate penalties, punishment needs to be made public in some way: in our own society, the media broadcast sufficient information about the activities of the police and the courts to give the general public at least some certainty that convicted criminals are being punished. Since the early nineteenth century, the industrial state has had the fiscal and human resources to provide a framework of overt and covert policing in even the least accessible parts of its territory, one of the effects of which is that it can be assumed, rightly or wrongly, that those who commit crimes will have to face a court of justice. The modern state also has the technical resources to maintain prisons that are at least reasonably escape-proof. Once someone has been convicted of a serious crime, there is considerable certainty that he will suffer deprivation of liberty on a scale thought to be roughly commensurate with the social harm he has done. The policeman and the prison are two visible factors that reassure a modern society that legal (if not moral) norms have more than just a theoretical role, and that ordinary people may carry on their lives on the assumption that those norms will be adhered to. When that reassurance is shattered as the result of a miscarriage of justice or an escape or threats by terrorists to commit further crimes unless a convicted associate is prematurely released from his punishment, then the reaction of the public is sometimes out of all proportion to the danger to public order which the particular incident itself poses. The focus of reassurance today is the trial; by contrast, the actual punishment has become almost a secret.

Extract (b)

The attack on gladiatorial games as 'despicable and defiled' by one of the earliest Greek apologists, Tatian, in the mid-second century, has to be seen as part of a wider attack on pagan rituals. Instances of objections to gladiatorial combat on the grounds found in Josephus, that it is shocking that men should suffer at Rome to give pleasure to others, are few in the extreme; the argument occurs in Prudentius' armoury of objections in his attack on the Vestal Virgins, but notwithstanding those who have wished to argue that Christians had a distinctively humanitarian approach to pain, it cannot there be taken seriously: Prudentius goes on to say that criminals should be sentenced to be killed by wild beasts instead. Any objections there may have been to the cruelty inflicted in the amphitheatre did not prevent Tertullian from seeing the Second Coming in terms of a spectacle: the mass execution of traitors, i.e. pagans, in a cosmic arena under the presidency of Christ. This was not a compassionate Christ, just as no compassion had been shown to those convicted of the crime of Christianity. Earlier Christian visions of the Last Judgement had been in terms of the destruction of an earthly city in warfare. For Roman Christians, the arena was an essential feature of the culture they shared with pagans, and the imagery of the arena, with its wild beasts, torture, burning, and weapons, provided Christians with some of the imagery for the picture of hell that was to persist through the centuries. The imagery of the arena was taken for granted by Christians, and some of them, as Romans, shared the belief that the arena was the place where a brave fighter achieves resurrection in the midst of death. The martyrs' bravery had overcome physical suffering in 'the contest of God, the battle of Christ'. Cyprian, bishop of Carthage in the AD 250s, exhorted those in danger of execution to remain steadfast in the faith.

The tortured showed more bravery than the torturers ... The blood which flowed might have sufficed to put out the fire of persecution, even to put out the flames of Gehenna with its glorious gore ... What a spectacle this was for the Lord – how sublime, how magnificent, how acceptable to God's eyes is the allegiance and devotion of his soldiers.

The metaphor of military bravery is strikingly applied to women martyrs in the *Passion of Perpetua and Felicity*. Their execution is represented as a battle against the devil in the Carthaginian arena; the president's box is occupied not by the proconsul, but by the Lord. Since Perpetua was a *honestior* [well-born citizen], her execution was in fact a swift one, by the sword: 'When the swordsman's hand shook (for he was only a trainee), Perpetua herself placed it in position on her neck.' The story of Perpetua's dream before her execution represents it as a gladiatorial contest, in which the martyr slays her opponent, a great black devil; for a Christian lady, playing the ambivalent figure of a gladiator might be as subconsciously attractive as for the pagan woman of high status satirized by Juvenal. The martyrs in ecstasy feel no physical pain:

Perpetua ... was so much in the ecstasy of the Spirit that she was like someone waking up from sleep; she started by looking round her, and then, to the surprise of everyone who was there, asked 'When are we to be thrown to the bull?' When she heard that this had already happened, she would not believe them, until she saw how her body and her clothing had been torn.

For the Roman hagiographer, the suffering of the saints does not matter because they are above ordinary mortality; a proposition which assumes that the sufferings of criminals, as witnessed year after year in the same amphitheatres, are to be taken for granted because they are below humanity.

The fact that Christian moralists had to point out the idolatrous associations of the arena again and again to their Christian readers over the centuries suggests that many or most Christians did not see them as sufficiently strong reasons for rejecting *munera* in theory, or staying away in practice. In the tract *On Spectacles*, Tertullian has to make the most of any pagan religious association that he can think of; this is one of the few ancient texts which explicitly explains the origins of *munera* as offerings to the *manes*, the souls of the deceased. Amphitheatres are pagan temples, dedicated to particular gods, and contain images of those gods. Victims are sacrificed to the underworld god Dis or Pluto. Two centuries later, Prudentius produced a particularly sustained critique of gladiatorial spectacles at the conclusion of his two long hexameter poems *Against Symmachus*. These literary essays were inspired by the publication at the end of the fourth century of the attack on the cult of the goddess Victory by St Ambrose, bishop of Milan from AD 374 to 397. Ambrose's letters were themselves a reply to an appeal in AD 384 to the emperor Valentinian by the orator Symmachus in his capacity as Urban Prefect, to allow the altar of Victory to be set up again in the Roman senate house, whence it had earlier been removed by Gratian. Symmachus' appeal had been rejected at the time, thanks largely to Ambrose's efforts. [...]

Prudentius clearly wants to see an end to gladiators as such, and not just the pagan religious associations of the arena. But his grounds are far from humanitarian as we would understand the term: 'Let no one fall dead in the City, whose punishment gives pleasure to others. Nor should girls' eyes take pleasure in killing. Let the ignoble arena be content with beasts alone; and let there be no man-killing games involving bloody weapons.'

The unease of Christians about *munera* is striking, and requires explanation. Certainly gladiatorial games had not become entirely 'secular', any more than other Roman spectacles. But Christian Rome and Byzantium found no difficulties in suppressing any pagan associations of chariot races and wild-beast shows and integrating these activities into a Christian polity. Prudentius did not perceive cruelty to criminals by using the *infamis arena*, the amphitheatre popular with the lower orders, for executions as a moral problem of any kind: on the contrary, he says that a city in which that happened would be devoted to God (*sit devota deo*, 2, 1130). The legislative enactments of Christian emperors from Constantine on show no inhibitions about extending the range of crimes calling for torture and execution by fire or wild beasts, as well as introducing more novel refinements such as the mutilation of various parts of the body used in committing particular crimes, and pouring molten lead down the throat of someone involved in the abduction of a virgin. There may be doubts about the extent to which late Roman criminal legislation was really more savage than that of the classical period, or merely reduced everyone apart from the elite to the level of judicial violence that had always been held for slaves and *dediticii* (rightless provincials).

C14 Keith Hopkins, Murderous games

From Keith Hopkins (1983) *Death and Renewal*, Cambridge, Cambridge University Press, pp.21–2.

The victorious gladiator, or at least his image, was sexually attractive. The word *gladius* – sword – was vulgarly used to mean penis. Even the defeated and dead gladiator had something sexually portentous about him. It was customary for a new bride to have her hair parted with a spear, at best one which had been dipped 'in the body of a defeated and killed gladiator' (Festus I.55 *sv caelibari hasta*). A stone relief from southern Italy (Beneventum) shows a heavily armed gladiator fighting a huge penis; besides him are written the words of the crowd: 'Free him. Kill him' (*missos iugula; CII.9.1671*). I am not at all sure how to interpret the significance of all this; such customs and artefacts can mean so many different things to different people, and even to the same person. But this evidence suggests that there was a close link, in some Roman minds, between gladiatorial fighting and sexuality.

All gladiators, whatever their formal status, received cash for winning, crowns for bravery, and if they were fortunate the wooden cudgel (*rudis*) as a symbol they need never fight in the arena again (Martial, *On the Public Shows* 29). The crowns were important. A painting from the amphitheatre at Pompeii, now lost, shows preparations for a gladiatorial combat; the gladiators are arming themselves, while in the background two winged figures of Victory hold out garlands for the prospective victor. And in graffiti at Pompeii, crude but touching line-drawings trace the outcome of gladiatorial fights; the contestants are identified by name, by the number of their fights or victories (it is now impossible to tell which) and sometimes by the number of crowns which they have won; for example:

| Hilarus of Nero's school | 14 fights 12 crowns | Won |
| Creunus | 7 fights 5 crowns | Discharged |

(CIL 4.10237)

Similarly, street advertisements for forthcoming shows put out by the producers and programmes (*libelli*), which spectators bought, listed combatants by gladiatorial type (*Thracian, Myrmillo, Hoplomachus* – all heavy-armed; *Essedarius* – chariot-fighter; *Retiarius* – light-armed Netter), and by previous record. In several graffiti, the outcome of the bouts was also noted. For example:

THRACIAN *vs* MYRMILLO

| Won | Pugnax of Nero's school | 3 fights |
| Killed | Murranus of Nero's school | 3 fights |

HOPLOMACHUS *vs* THRACIAN

| Won | Cycnus of the Julian school | 8 fights |
| Discharged | Atticus of the Julian school | 14 fights ... |

CHARIOT-FIGHTERS

| Discharged | P. Ostorius | 51 fights |
| Won | Scylax of the Julian school | 26 fights |

(CIL 4.2508)

Without the results this reads, I suggest, like a guide to form. Spectators needed to know the combatants' capacity to survive and their experience, as a guide to betting (Ovid, *The Art of Love* 1.168). The emotional glue of Roman gladiatorial shows, what drew the crowd, was not merely the spectacle and the slaughter, but also gambling.

Why did Romans popularize fights to the death between armed gladiators? Why did they encourage the public slaughter of unarmed criminals? What was it, asked Tertullian, which transformed men who were timid and peaceable enough in private and made them shout gleefully for the merciless destruction of their fellow men (*On the Public Shows* 21)? Part of the answer may lie in the social psychology of the crowd, which helps relieve the individual of responsibility, and in the psychological mechanisms by which some spectators identify more readily with the victory of the aggressor than with the sufferings of the vanquished. Slavery and the steep stratification of society must have helped. Slaves were at the mercy of their owners. Those who were destroyed for public edification and entertainment were considered worthless (cf. Tacitus, *Annals* 1.76), as non-persons; or like the Christian martyrs, they were considered social outcasts and were tortured as if 'we no longer existed' (Eusebius, *History of the Church* 8.10). The brutalization of the audience fed on the dehumanization of the victims.

C15 G. Jennison, Animals for show and pleasure in Ancient Rome

From G. Jennison (1937) *Animals for Show and Pleasure in Ancient Rome*, Manchester, pp.66–9.

[N]o subsequent exhibitions were ever on the scale of those of Pompey and Caesar. At Pompey's games there were, as recorded, 17 or 18 elephants, 500 or 600 lions, 410 other African animals; and at Caesar's 400 lions and 40 elephants. But the exhibition of hundreds of lions and bears and African animals at spectacles, not to speak of larger numbers of commoner animals, was, according to the imperial historians, by no means rare. According to Augustus' own statement, who took especial delight in 'untold numbers and unknown shapes of beasts', 500 African animals alone were laid low in the spectacles he provided. At the hundred days' festival given by Titus at the dedication of the Flavian amphitheatre in 80 AD, on one day 5,000 wild animals of various sorts were exhibited, and 9,000 tame and wild was the sum total of the killed and, at the four months' festival of Trajan in 107 AD at the second Dacian triumph, 11,000.

The animals, consumed at Rome for one great festival, would amply stock all the Zoological Gardens of modern Europe. Science also profited of this profusion. According to Galen, physicians assembled at the dissection of a large elephant; the heart was taken out by the imperial cooks. Drugs were also concocted out of the parts of wild animals. Artists also studied their shapes; the famous sculptor, Pasitales, a contemporary of Pompey, was one day modelling a lion in one cage, when a panther escaped out of an adjoining cage, and he barely escaped with his life.

But *venationes* [beast hunts] were also given, throughout the empire, in the minor towns, and the demand for wild animals must have necessitated incessant hunts within and without the empire, to provide them for the emperors and private individuals, whether providers of festivals or merchants. These hunts went on for centuries, and the parents had to be killed, in order to capture the whelps; hence, the animal kingdom became wholly transformed, wild animals extirpated and driven into wildernesses, and new ground gained for civilization and agriculture.

Even in Strabo's time the ground between Carthage and the Columns of Hercules had been so far extirpated that the nomads could turn to agriculture; and could defend themselves against them, partly because they were proficient huntsmen, and the Roman passion for *venationes* supported them.

'Oh distant Nasamonian Lands of the Libyans', says a Greek poet, 'your barren plains are no longer visited by flocks of beasts of prey, you no longer tremble at the lion's roaring in the desert; for Caesar has caught a vast number of them, in nets, for one single exhibition, and the former lofty lairs of wild beasts are now pasturages.'

Thus, too, the needs of the Roman amphitheatre relieved the cornfields of Egypt from the ravages of the hippopotami, which were common in Pliny's time above the Praefecture of Sais, and, in the fourth century, had been banished to the upper reaches of Nubia. A writer of the fourth century regrets that there are no more elephants in Libya, or lions in Thessaly, or hippopotami in the swamps of the Nile. Now hippopotami are no longer found even in Nubia, and occur commonly only in the Eastern Sudan and the heart of Africa.

Thus, in antiquity, the hunting-ground in Africa became exhausted; but Asia was still prolific in wild animals, with which the kings and satraps of Persia reinforced their menageries, and supplied those of the Roman Emperors of the fourth century, who laid out their own after the same model. Even in Ammianus' times in the reeds and jungles of Mesopotamia there were 'countless' lions, and in Hyrcania swarms of tigers and other wild animals. At the frontiers of the empire, there was an import tax on all Asiatic products, as on animals intended for spectacles, such as 'Indian (i.e. Asiatic) lions, pards, leopards and panthers'. Symmachus calculates the harbour-tolls on beasts at 2 per cent, from which senatorial givers of festivals were exempted. [...]

The wealth of the imperial menageries and gardens in the rarest and most costly animals may be estimated from the catalogue of those at Rome under Gordian III: 32 elephants, 10 elks, 10 tigers, 60 tame lions, 30 tame leopards, 10 hyaenas, 1 rhinoceros, 1 hippopotamus, [...], 10 giraffes, 20 wild asses, 40 wild horses, and countless other animals, all of which Philip devoted to the millenary celebrations of 248 AD. The administration and upkeep of these menageries involved a large staff, and a large annual outlay: once, when meat was dear, Caligula fed them with criminals; Aurelian sold those used at his triumph to save the fisc [treasury] the cost of their keep. Besides the imperial menageries (for which purpose the extensive vaults of the Church of San Giovanni e Paolo may in part have served) there were others in Rome. In the third century the Praetorian and City cohorts owned a menagerie, possible the *vivarium* mentioned by Procopius, near the Praenestine Gate (*porta maggiore*) just outside the wall, near the *amphitheatrum castrense* [camp amphitheatre], which also belonged to them. In the imperial gardens animals may also have been kept, as, for instance, in a park by Nero's Golden House.

Probably the emperors often gave their friends and privileged senators animals for amphitheatrical shows. Symmachus received for his son's Praetorian Games from Honorius, at Stilicho's request, a gift of several leopards. Further, Roman grandees generally owned land in Africa and Asia, and could utilize the friendship of the provincial governors, and thus expedite the importation of animals; but the Republican practice of making contributions of money and wild animals to the spectacles of the procurator's friends a permanent tax on the provincials, had fallen into disuse. The higher Roman officials had come to regard the supplying of wild animals as a trifling and matter-of-course act of friendliness on the part of the provincial procurator, as Cicero's letters when proconsul in Cilicia in 51 BC from Marcus Caelius the aedile [public official] show. 'Patiscus', Caelius writes, 'has sent Curio ten panthers; it would be a shame, should Cicero not send more; he need only issue the commission; food and transport had been provided'. As a return-favour was exceedingly probable, such requests were not lightly refused.

Thus, thousands of brave huntsmen, year in, year out, ran dangers in every zone, to furnish the demand of the amphitheatre for animals. For one great Roman festival, with due Roman splendour, the Hindu tamed elephants to catch elephants, the Rhinelanders spread nets over the boars in the reeds, Moors on their hardy ponies encircled ostriches in the deserts, and lurked in the horrible solitudes of the Atlas by the lion-pits. Should these perilous ventures succeed, devices for transport called a new industry into being. The axe rang and the saw grated, the anvil grew hot; and at last the terrible captives vented their rage on the bars of their cages. Claudian in his poem on Stilicho describes a *venatio* given by him. To honour his patron, Diana and all her nymphs hunted in the forests, the wildernesses and the hills of the world, the carpenters had not wood enough to make even all the beams; and cages had to be made, with box and elm wood still green, and the leaves visible.

Transport was effected mostly by sea, and storms might delay or wreck: there were at the wharves of the Campus Martius in the late Republic cages for the temporary safeguarding of animals. But long trains of heavy ox-wagons loaded with cages also came by land. The huge distances often necessitated voyages of many months, in which the animals might succumb to death or disease. An Edict of Honorius and Theodosius obliges towns through which imperial transport of animals passed to provide for their provision; probably this only regularized pre-existing practice. This decision led to great abuses, for an edict was issued by these two emperors that no such stay should exceed seven days, for one such train dallied in Hierapolis, the capital of the province of the Euphrates, for three to four months, and the conductors, contrary to all precedent, required cages as well to be supplied.

In the amphitheatre the animals were hunted, made to fight one another, and let loose on men: but some few harmless and rarer sorts were only paraded. They used to be decorated as though for a sacrifice or procession.

C16   K.M. Coleman, Fatal charades

From K.M. Coleman (1990) 'Fatal charades: Roman executions staged as mythological enactments', *Journal of Roman Studies*, vol.LXXX, 1990, pp.44–73, extracts from pp.64, 67, 73.

We do know that one of the means whereby Nero added an element of *ludibrium* (sport) to his public execution of Christians was by clothing some in animal-skins before having them thrown to dogs (Tacitus, *Annals*. 15.44.4: 'et pereuntibus addita ludibria, ut ferarum tergis contecti laniatu canum interirent'). Perhaps 'Pasiphae' was enveloped in cow-hide. The most effective method of rousing taurine lust, however, would be to smear upon the woman's genitalia the vaginal secretions of a cow in season.[1] Were she a condemned prisoner, it would obviously not matter if her internal organs were damaged in such an enactment; indeed, the expectation is that she would be killed, if not in the encounter with the bull then dispatched afterwards by the sword. Thus Apuleius' *Golden Ass*, shown by Fergus Millar[2] to be a faithful representation of many aspects of contemporary life, may in one of its most Rabelaisian scenes be less fanciful than is usually supposed: the female poisoner condemned *ad bestias*, who had been bought up by the local magistrate, is due to perform intercourse with Lucius in his asinine form in front of the audience at Corinth (Apuleius, *Metamorphoses* 10.29.34). The *frisson* to be felt by the readers here is not, then, engendered so much by the prospect of a woman engaged in an act of bestiality as by the dramatic irony that her partner in this shocking scene is actually another human being in disguise.

Apart from Mucius Scaevola, all the examples of fatal charades that we have examined so far have come from Greek myth. A near-contemporary Roman legend that achieved great popularity forms the plot of the fourth 'charade' documented in the *Liber Spectaculorum*. The story of the bandit-leader Laureolus, who was eventually put to death after a successful career, formed the plot of a well-known mime, powerfully endorsing the triumph of authority over lawlessness. The earliest recorded performance (under Gaius) is mentioned by both Josephus and Suetonius because on this occasion the realism was grossly overdone: when 'Laureolus' had to vomit blood, the supporting actors tried so hard to rival his efforts that the whole stage was awash. It appears from Josephus (*Jewish Antiquities* 19. 94) and Juvenal (*Satires* 8. 188) that traditionally Laureolus died by crucifixion: Juvenal observes that it is so scandalous to see a Roman gentleman acting the part of Laureolus in a mime that he deserves real crucifixion, *dignus vera cruce*.

This realism could be achieved in the amphitheatre; but when his story is enacted in the arena, Laureolus' death acquires a bizarre twist: he is mauled by a bear (Martial, *Book of Shows.* 7): [...]

IV. Myth and autocracy

In conclusion I shall attempt to address two questions: how did punishment come to be enacted in the context of mythological role-play, and why is it that most of the evidence is clustered in the latter half of the first century AD? My suggested answers are but tentative, and intended to provoke discussion.

(a)   Mythological role-play

In a society where mythology was the cultural currency, the ritual events of ordinary life might naturally be set in a mythological context; to put it more broadly, Greco-Roman mythology provided an all-encompassing frame of reference for everyday Roman experience. A superficial appropriateness was quite adequate; points of detail did not have to correspond.

When Q. Hortensius picnicked with his guests in the game-park (*therothrophium*) on his estate near Laurentum, 'Orpheus' would be in attendance, decked out in robes and holding a lyre; when the signal was given (on a horn, as a concession to practical considerations),[3] stags and boars would flock round 'Orpheus' (to be fed) as though charmed by his fabulous music (Varro, *de Re Rustica.* 3.13.2–3). Trimalchio's ignorance of mythological detail might force Daedalus to shut Niobe inside the Trojan Horse,[4] but in everyday matters he could exploit mythological prototypes: the slave who handed round grapes at table played the role of Bacchus in his various aspects (Petronius, *Satyricon* 41.6); the veal that was served after an interlude of Homeric recitation was, appropriately enough, sliced by 'Ajax', who slashed at it in a feigned frenzy that belied his expertise at carving (*Satyricon* 59.7). A phenomenon that began in Rome under Claudius and Nero, and remained largely confined to Italy and the western provinces, was the practice among slaves and freedmen of decorating funerary monuments with scenes in which deities and mythological characters were portrayed in the likeness of the deceased; scant regard was paid to the consequences of pursuing the mythological identification, so that (for example) a faithful wife could be portrayed as Alcestis without implying her suicide.

In this climate of thought, the outcome of fatal encounters in the amphitheatre was predictably ritualized in terms of the transition of the underworld:[5] 'Larvae' hounded cowardly recruits, 'Mercury' prodded corpses with a brand to test their lifelessness, and 'Pluto' accompanied the bodies out of the arena. Yet this allegorizing interpretation of the amphitheatre does not require that those who die in the arena should do so in the role of famous characters from mythology, since the underworld catered for everyone and not only for mythological heroes. Indeed, it is clearly exceptional for displays in the amphitheatre to be cast as mythological enactments. But we can at least say that the cultural consciousness that interpreted the amphitheatre as the threshold of the underworld might infuse encounters in the arena with the same timeless mythological atmosphere.

A contemporary attitude that must have been significant in shaping the expectations of audiences is revealed by the stress our sources lay upon the actuality of what is being enacted in these fatal charades. 'Seeing is believing': 'accepit fabula prisca fidem' is Martial's comment on the spectacle of 'Pasiphae' mating with the bull (*Book of Shows* 5.2). Myth has been vindicated by the reality of 'here and now'. 'Laureolus', 'non falsa pendens in cruce' [Laureolus hanging on a real cross], did in reality suffer the fate ascribed to him in legend: 'quae fuerat fabula, poena fuit' [what had been a play became a punishment] (*Book of Shows* 7.12). [...]

Titus' inauguration of the Flavian Amphitheatre was perhaps rather a dedication of his extensions to it; Vespasian may well have inaugurated the first three storeys, completed in his own lifetime. Titus' celebration must have made a striking impact after the disasters of volcanic eruption, fire and plague.[6] Whatever ceremony Vespasian may have held was completely eclipsed by Titus' one hundred days of extravagant displays.

The survival of evidence so particular as to mention charades of this nature is a matter of chance that makes it especially hazardous to draw inferences about the recurrence of such displays. We should recall that for Titus' magnificent *ludi* Suetonius and Dio yield the conventional statistics about participants and casualties, while Martial alone supplies evidence for the gruesome mythological enactments on the programme. Hence, while it seems safe to say that surviving testimony coincides with a period in which the Principate was being stripped of its mask of constitutional legitimacy to reveal the autocratic imperial authority beneath, in later reigns the silence of Dio and the *Historia Augusta* cannot be taken as proof that such displays had altogether ceased at Rome. In one province, at least, we know that such enactments were being performed at the end of the second century: although the Christians' monotheistic fanaticism would make them obvious targets for this type of punishment, Tertullian's remark, 'in cavea ... ipsos deos vestros saepe noxii induunt' [in the arena the guilty often take on the guise of the gods themselves], implies neither that this treatment was exclusively reserved for Christians nor that it was especially rare. Indeed, ambitious provincial magistrates further afield than North Africa may have reinforced their own authority and boosted their reputations by so dramatizing, on occasion, the humdrum reality of capital punishment.

The amphitheatre was where one went to witness and participate in a spectacle of death: the death of animals and men, specifically the deaths of worthless and harmful persons. Whatever the crises of an emperor's reign and threats to the stability of his regime, there were people and animals available for sacrifice who, by dying violently, would earn his popular acclaim and demonstrate his authority over life and death. What makes our charades unique in the history of the *ludi* is the mythological context in which they were performed: to witness the enactment of myth here was to experience not escapism but reality, and the emperor who verified myth worked a miracle. Justice was seen to be done, and the death of the criminal was all the more degrading for the short-lived glamour of his mythological role. The wealth and ingenuity and benevolence of the sponsor; the heights of realism achieved by the technological wonders of the arena; the rapidly expanding category of persons subject to the harsher treatments in a differentiated system of penalties; the co-operation of a body of spectators who were used to violence and admired novelty – all these factors combined to interpret reality as myth, thereby translating myth into reality: *accepit fabula prisca fidem* [an ancient story received verification].

[1] The woman may even have been tied onto the bull. The key word is *iunctam* (I), common diction for sexual intercourse.

[2] 'The world of the *Golden Ass*', *Journal of Roman Studies* 71 (1981), 6375.

[3] Apparently a standard procedure, since Varro's game-keeper (not in fancy-dress) blew a horn to summon boars and deer to be fed (*RR*. 3.13.1).

[4] Petronius, *Satyricon* 52.2.

[5] cf. the practice in medieval Italy of displaying pictures of Hell to condemned prisoners en route to their places of execution, to concentrate their attention upon their fate.

[6] Dedicated March/April 80 (*CIL* vi. 2059), i.e. after the eruption of Vesuvius (August 79) and resulting plague: the fire occured in 80, but admittedly perhaps not until summer when Rome was at its most combustible (i.e. during or after Titus' games).

ACKNOWLEDGEMENTS

Grateful acknowledgement is made to the following sources for permission to reproduce material in this book:

Text

A57 and A58: Hardy, T. 'A Church Romance' and 'Hap', *The Collected Poems of Thomas Hardy*, 1965, Papermac; A63: 'Leda and the Swan', reprinted with the permission of Simon and Schuster, Inc. from *The Collected Works of W. B. Yeats, Volume 1: The Poems*, revised and edited by Richard J. Finnerman. Copyright 1928 by Macmillan Publishing Company; copyright renewed © 1956 by Georgie Yeats, and by permission of A.P. Watt Ltd; A65 and A66: McKay, C. 'The White House' and 'If we must die', used by permission of The Archives of Claude McKay, Carl Cowl, Administrator; A67: 'What lips my lips have kissed' by Edna St Vincent Millay, from *Collected Poems*, HarperCollins. Copyright 1923, 1951 by Edna St Vincent Millay. All rights reserved. Reprinted by permission of Elizabeth Barnett, literary executor; A68 and A69: Owen, W. 'Anthem for Doomed Youth' and Hospital Barge at Cérisy' from Stallworthy, J. (ed.) *The Poems of Wilfred Owen*, 1963, Chatto and Windus Ltd and the Executors of Harold Owen's Estate. Reprinted also by permission of New Directions Publishing Corp.; A71: Reprinted by permission of The Peters Fraser and Dunlop Group Limited on behalf of Blunden, E. 1930, 'Vlamertinghe: Passing the Château, July, 1917', *Poems 1914–30*, Cobden/Sanderson; A72 and A73: Excerpts from 'Altarwise by owl-light' by Dylan Thomas, from *The Poems of Dylan Thomas*. Copyright © 1939 by New Directions Publishing Corp.. Reprinted by permission of New Directions Publishing Corp. and David Higham Associates Limited; A74 and A75: Brooks, G. © 1991, 'First fight. Then fiddle' and 'What shall I give my children' from *Blacks* published by Third World Press, Chicago; A76: Magee, J. 'High Flight', *The Complete Works of John Magee The Pilot Poet*, 1989, This England Books; A77: Excerpts from 'Tales of the Islands' from *Collected Poems 1948–1984* by Derek Walcott. Copyright © 1986 by Derek Walcott. Reprinted by permission of Farrar, Straus & Giroux, Inc. and Faber and Faber Ltd; A78: Thomas, R. S. 1967, 'Composition', *Poetry for Supper*, Rupert Hart-Davis, by permission of the author; A79 and A80: Excerpts from Morgan, E. 'Glasgow Sonnets', *Poems of Thirty Years*, 1982, Carcanet Press Limited; A81: Dunn, D. 1985, 'A Silver Air Force', *Elegies*, Faber and Faber Ltd; A82 and A83: Dunn, D. 'Kaleidoscope' and 'Sandra's Mobile', *Selected Poems 1964–1983*, 1986, Faber and Faber Ltd; A84, A85, A86 and A87: Harrison, T. 1981, 'On Not Being Milton', 'Them & [uz]', 'Book Ends' and 'Continuous', *Continuous: 50 Sonnets from The School of Eloquence*, by permission of Gordon Dickerson; A88, A89 and A90: excerpts from 'Clearances' from *The Haw Lantern* by Seamus Heaney. Reprinted by permission of Farrar, Straus & Giroux, Inc. and Faber and Faber Ltd; A91:

Cope, W. 1992, 'Faint Praise', *Serious Concerns*, Faber and Faber Ltd; A92: Cope, W. 'Strugnell's Bargain' with the author's permission; A93: Cope, W. 'The Sitter' in Collins, J. and Lindner, E. (eds) *Writing on the Wall*, Weidenfeld and Nicolson, with the permission of The Orion Publishing Group; A94: Gioia, D., 1986, 'Sunday Night in Santa Rosa', *Daily Horoscope*, Windover Press Inc.

B4: Warburton, N., 1995, *Philosophy: The Basics*, 2nd edition, Routledge; B5: Rachels, J. 'Active and passive euthanasia', reprinted by permission of *The New England Journal of Medicine*, 292, pp. 78–80, copyright © 1975 Massachusetts Medical Society.

C1: Reprinted by permission of Harvard Business School. An excerpt from *Martial Epigrams*, Volume 1, translated by Shackleton, D. R., edited by Gould, G. P., Copyright © 1993, by the President and Fellows of Harvard College; all rights reserved; C9: Seneca, translated by Costa, C. D. N. 1988, *17 Letters*, Aris-Phillips; C10: Baldick, R. (ed.) 1961, *St Augustine, Confessions*, translated by Pine Coffin, R. S., Penguin Books Ltd; C11: Weidermann, T. 1991, 'Emperors, Gladiators, Christians', *Omnibus*, 22, September 1991, JACT, and with permission of the author; C12: Pearson, J. 1973, *Arena: The Story of the Colosseum*, McGraw-Hill Inc., by permission of the McGraw-Hill Group; C13 (a) and (b): Wiedemann, T. 1992, *Emperors and Gladiators*, Routledge; C14: Hopkins, K. 1983, *Death and Renewal*, Cambridge University Press; C15: Jennison, G. 1937, *Animals for Show And Pleasure in Ancient Rome*, Manchester University Press; C16: Coleman, K. M. 1990, 'Fatal charades: Roman executions staged as mythical enactments', *Journal of Roman Studies*, LXXX, Society for the Promotion of Roman Studies.

Figures

C11: Figure 1: Courtesy of A. F. Kersting; Figure 2: Courtesy of Bildarchiv Foto Marburg; Figure 3: Courtesy of the Ancient Art and Architecture Library, London.